THE GREAT JAZZ REVIVAL

A Pictorial Celebration of Traditional Jazz

by
Jim Goggin & Peter Clute
with an introduction by
Philip Elwood
edited by
Donna Ewald & Umberto Tosi

Donna Ewald, Publisher

This book is dedicated to

Jim's Daughter Carol

and Pete's Daughter Aphra

...because we miss them.

First Edition
Copyright© 1994 by
Jim Goggin and Peter Clute.
All rights reserved.
No part of this book may be
reproduced in any form
without written permission
from the publisher.

Printed in Sacramento
by Griffin Printing

ISBN: 0-9641067-0-1

Library of Congress
Catalog Card Number:
94-71239

Book and cover design:
Raymond Moreno of MAX

Donna Ewald, Publisher
1537 4th Street #43
San Rafael, California 94901

Front cover: Cartoon of the YBJB by Clark Wright courtesy of Maria and Al Haas.

Back cover: James P. Johnson at Hambone Kelly's. This photo, from the Charles Campbell collection, captures the prevailing spirit of the Great Jazz Revival in the 40s. On the trombone was Joe Zohn, the trumpet player was Eddie Smith and on bass, Pat Patton. Others we can identify in the photo include Patsy Patton (next to Pat), and Dick Oxtot (under trombone slide).

CONTENTS

ACKNOWLEDGEMENTS 4

FOREWORD by Peter Clute and Jim Goggin 5

INTRODUCTION by Philip Elwood 6

THE 30S AND BEFORE
THE BIRTH, DEATH AND REVIVAL OF EARLY JAZZ *10*

THE 40S
THE REVIVAL THRIVES *24*

THE 50S
TWO–BEAT GOES ON *60*

THE 60S
DIFFERENT DRUMMERS: TRAD JAZZ SPREADS *92*

THE 70S 80S 90S AND TOMORROW
TRAD JAZZ MARCHES TO THE MILLENNIUM *112*

SELECTED BIBLIOGRAPHY 158

RECORDINGS 159

AUTHOR'S BIOGRAPHIES 160

ACKNOWLEDGEMENTS

A couple of years ago, while looking at some wonderful jazz photographs, Donna Ewald remarked "you two should write a book about jazz". Since she had just organized and written a book (with Peter Clute) SAN FRANCISCO INVITES THE WORLD (Chronicle Books, 1991) she was well aware of what it takes to complete such a project.

So this triad of friends agreed to work on a book about the revival of traditional jazz. Our roles were to obtain material and write what we thought would be interesting. Donna's role as co-editor and publisher was to make the book a reality and that is exactly what she did. She made sure we kept to a schedule and arranged for the necessary art, printing and financial help. Along with our brilliant co-editor, Umberto Tosi, she expanded the captions and text and added information where necessary. Her mother, Helen Ewald, helped her sort through the photographs – a tough job as the authors could not bear to cut one photo! Donna worked closely with the talented Laura Lamar and Raymond Moreno of MAX who did a superb job of design and layout.

The next step was the acquisition of suitable material which was made easier because of the existence of the non-profit corporation, the San Francisco Traditional Jazz Foundation. With some exceptions, most of the material in this book is the property of the Foundation and without their kindness we could not have completed our work. Any questions you might have about records or books or if you just want to make a donation, as we did, of cash, books, records etc. just write (enclosing an addressed, stamped envelope) to:

> Bill Carter, San Francisco Traditional Jazz Foundation
> 650 California Street 12th Floor
> San Francisco, CA 94108

It's a nice way to say " thanks " for all the enjoyment jazz has given you.

We are indebted to Herb Caen for his gracious comment on our back cover, and also for allowing us to quote his wonderful columns throughout the book. And a big thank you to Philip Elwood, a true jazz fan, for his marvelous introduction. It meant a great deal to us to have Bob Helm, the gifted musician, agree to contribute. His writings formed a big portion of the introductions to the 30s, 40s, and 50s sections. He was also helpful in setting us straight on facts and figures. We must acknowledge K. O. Eckland, the author of Jazz West 1945 to 1985, whose unpublished paper, The Southland Swings, is excerpted here. Charles Campbell and Maria Haas were a tremendous help. These two jazz afficionados had many wonderful memories to share.

Others we sincerely want to thank are:
*Maria Goggin and Carol Clute for encouragement throughout
*Laverne Ballou (Monte's widow)
*Roxie and Jeff Goggin for allowing us the "use of their hall"
*Joan Hayes (Clancy's daughter-in-law and the widow of Bill Hayes)
*Harry Mordecai
*Mark Parode
*Don Ewald for his idea for the cover
*Kay Helm
*3PM Corporation
*Evan Hansen
*Laura Cirolia for design in-put way back when
*Ada and Henry Shirek. Ada was a jazz fan who saved hundreds of clippings about local jazz musicians. Her collection was donated to the Foundation after her death by her husband Henry
*Sharon Deveaux, Deveaux Photographics
*Errol Hall, B&W Color Images, for stepping in and getting the photos done so beautifully – and quickly
*Harry Avery, who knew so much about jazz
*Vicki Morgan
*George Tyler for so many reasons
*All the marvelous photographers, known and unknown who had the foresight to record history. Special thank you to Ed Lawless who never failed to help us out. (Dottie, too)
*Bill Tooley , Chuck Huggins and Greg Peterson - Avid jazz fans and enthusiastic supporters of the project. This book would not have been completed, or even attempted, without them. We hope they know how much their support meant to us and all the jazz fans who will read this book
*The incomparable Wally Rose
*And of course, Turk Murphy

If we have forgotten anyone, it was not intentional. Finally, we want to thank you for buying our book. We sincerely hope our love for the past and present musicians who spent their lives making the world a better place, is revealed within the pages of THE GREAT JAZZ REVIVAL

J.G. & P.C.

FOREWORD

by Peter Clute & Jim Goggin

It is my hope that assembling this book will encourage and illuminate those of you interested in West Coast Jazz. What is it? Who started it? Why is it special? These are questions I once had...

When I was thirteen, just after the end of WWII, my brother Cedric introduced me to West Coast Jazz. Of course it wasn't known by that name then. Like so many events that shape the course of a person's life, that introduction set me on a life's path of work and pleasure based on what we now call "traditional jazz".

Traditional jazz is an ensemble style of playing. The individual members each have a definite part to play. The cornet or trumpet has the lead, the clarinet plays a third above the cornet, the trombone a fifth below. In the rhythm section, the tuba plays the first and third beats, the banjo (or guitar) the second and fourth and the piano fills in the holes. The drums keep a beat and are meant to be heard mainly by the band members.

This is a simple sketch of a two-beat West Coast style band. As a young player becomes proficient at his trade, his vistas expand. The ultimate sensual pleasure of ensemble playing is the whole band "locked -in" when all the parts become one.

It's not a difficult concept to understand, but it doesn't happen all the time. You'll know when it happens.

In the late 40s and early 50s we had Dixieland, New York, Chicago and New Orleans jazz. People would ask "what kind of music do you play?" It became apparent that the style of music on the West Coast was different than that played even in New Orleans. We needed to find a word in keeping with the roots of New Orleans style jazz. "Traditional" seemed to fit the bill as it referred to the music which came out of New Orleans around the turn-of-the-century when most of the musicians left to find jobs, better wages and better bands in the northern cities such as Chicago and New York. These places also had radio and recording studios.

West Coast Jazz was termed "revival" as it was an effort to bring attention to a music neglected for years which even in its beginning was not widely known.

The true test of the lasting power of any form of artistic endeavor is its end product. Although most traditional jazz is now performed at jazz festivals rather than nightclubs, there is a growing knowledge of it throughout the world. It is played by bands in France, Germany, Sweden, Denmark, Italy, Spain, Poland, Czechoslovakia, Russia, Japan, Brazil, Canada, Hong Kong, Australia...there are more bands playing West Coast Jazz now than at any other time in the past! Guess I can keep working for some time...

Peter Clute

We'll take you on a pictorial journey from the depression of the 30s through the Golden Gate Exposition of 1939, WWII, the 1950s, 60s, 70s, and up through today. We hope to encourage both existing and new fans to keep playing and listening to West Coast Jazz. Although extensive, the pictures encompassing the body of this book are but a glimpse of the last 60 years. Editing the collection for publication was a painful process as there was so much great material to choose from! I had the privilege of collecting most of this memorabilia throughout the years - it is now in the hands of the fine San Francisco Traditional Jazz Foundation.

We wrote this book for those of you who want to know about the Great Jazz Revival. What was it like to be a working musician in the 30s and 40s? Who was in the original Yerba Buena Jazz Band? These questions and many others needed to be answered.

I want to give a special salute to Bob Helm, who was kind enough to contribute to our book. He is a superb musician, a good writer and importantly HE WAS THERE. Bob shared with Turk Murphy and Lu Watters a desire to get away from playing the same tunes exactly the same way everytime. Both Pete and I feel that Bob has not gotten the credit he deserves. Just listen to the West Coast label recordings and you will agree that Bob's "signature" helped to make the sound of the Yerba Buena Jazz Band so distinctive.

Those of you who came to Earthquake McGoon's will remember the reclining nude above the bar - a raised shotglass in her hand. The picture was a blow up of an old whiskey ad, done for Pete and Turk by "Evil Andy" White who now lives in Hawaii. The nude became known as Mother McGoon and the plaque on the picture reads "It's Up To You". So, because we could only use a small number of the photographs and mementoes from the collection in this book, if you want more (as Mother McGoon would say) "It's Up To You"!

Jim Goggin

INTRODUCTION

by Philip Elwood

Take One of Two

For the past half century documenters of jazz history have unfairly and unwisely dismissed the San Francisco-based (and ultimately worldwide) traditional jazz revival of the late 1940s as a reactionary, imitative musical movement which ran counter to bebop and other "progressive" modern jazz sounds. Even the better writings which deal with west coast jazz activities in the post-World War II era focus almost entirely on the Los Angeles modern jazz scene (which acquired the generic title of "West Coast Jazz") while concurrently bemoaning the absence of jazz in the San Francisco area.

There was, of course, a San Francisco jazz style— a powerful, compelling, eclectic music which gradually got its act together in various ad hoc groups during the 1930s.

By 1940 a number of these dedicated San Francisco instrumentalists had organized under trumpeter Lu Watters as the Yerba Buena Jazz Band.

Most of the early jazz tunes in the Yerba Buena Band's book were familiar to swing-era fans, such as Louis Armstrong, the Bob Crosby Bob Cats, Woody Herman's Orchestra, the Count Basie Band and the many Original Dixieland Jazz Band offshoots.

As a young teenage junkshop record collector I thought I knew most of the 1920s jazz tunes but at my first encounter with the Yerba Buena Jazz Band— a meeting at the Dawn Club of the S.F. Jazz Society in the fall of 1940— I heard some marvelously attractive numbers unknown to me, played with an urgent lustiness that I found overwhelming.

And I still do.

Since the Watters band played a considerable number of tunes associated with Jelly Roll Morton, King Oliver, Louis Armstrong and other New Orleans musicians, its style was loosely defined as "New Orleans Jazz." Later the Yerba Buena Band's trombonist Turk Murphy would come to use the term "traditional jazz" to define the music his post-Watters band played.

In retrospect, I think we should have given Watters, Murphy, clarinetist Bob Helm, trumpeter Bob Scobey, pianists Wally Rose, Burt Bales and Paul Lingle, the banjoist-vocalist Clancy Hayes and their many colleagues more proper due by calling the Yerba Buena Band's music "San Francisco Jazz".

And we should now, as we should have then, been proud of those qualities which distinguished it from all other jazz band sounds.

San Francisco's popular music, including whatever "jazz" came its way, had long contained unique elements. Like New Orleans, San Francisco was a major seaport, a mercantile center, a businessman's party town and a sailor's shoreleave favorite.

Frisco's "Barbary Coast" zone during the turn of the century's ragtime era was certainly as infamous as New Orleans' "Storyville" district from whence, as the story goes, jazz emerged.

The 1906 earthquake and fire destroyed the rowdy Barbary Coast zone, although judging from all reports and research San Francisco's music scene - legit and illegit - continued on a high-gear roll right on into the 1920s.

Watters, Murphy, Rose, Helm and others in the Yerba Buena Band were native northern Californians steeped in the musical traditions of the area, outdoors and indoors. Ragtime band tunes (including vaudeville numbers like *Didn't He Ramble*), cowboy-country songs, barrelhouse piano ragtime, syncopated Dixieland danceband tunes and a smattering of "hot jazz" numbers were all part of the San Francisco Jazz sound-mix.

The Bay Area's small Negro community was primarily in Oakland, the western railhead for the transcontinental passenger and freight lines. It was in Oakland that the Kid Ory Band from New Orleans (via Los Angeles) played in the early 1920s and it was in Oakland that black railroad employees brought 1920s jazz and blues recordings back from Chicago.

And it was in the Oakland area (across the bay from San Francisco) that the Yerba Buena Jazz Band formed, the product of late night rehearsal/jam sessions held in an Oakland hills roadhouse.

The Yerba Buena Band became the weekend house band at downtown San Francisco's basement Dawn Club in December of 1940. The joint's leftover speakeasy atmosphere, big dance floor, downtown location and low prices made it a favorite alternative nightspot (the Palace Hotel was next door) for the college-age

left

Turk Murphy and Phil Elwood at KPFA Radio circa 1950s. Phil, a life-long resident of Berkeley, began broadcasting jazz programs in the late 1940s and has been a jazz program producer at radio KPFA FM, Berkeley, since 1952. He became the San Francisco Examiner's jazz critic in 1965 and for 35 years has taught American History and American Music History at the college level throughout the Bay Area.

crowd as well as the ever increasing number of anti-swing, traditional jazz fans and record collectors.

"NO TUNE PLAYED WRITTEN AFTER 1929" The Dawn Club matchbooks read — but what wasn't said was that all the tunes that were played were done in Lu Watters' San Francisco style — two trumpets, trombone and clarinet carrying the instrumental lead and two banjos, tuba, drums and piano thrashing out the strong rhythm.

It was a brassy, heavy-beat sound, yet the Watters band did swing in a muscular way, and it did have a spirit and good humor — musically and individually.

In 1941 the San Francisco Bay Area's hotel supperclubs, ballrooms and theaters were featuring all the nation's popular swing and dance bands, the Fillmore district (center of the expanding black community) had some modern swing clubs with excellent combos and Annie Street had Lu Watters and the Yerba Buena Jazz Band.

Who could have foreseen that by the end of the decade (with World War II in the middle) it would be the traditional older sounds of Lu Watters and the Yerba Buena Jazz Band that would be called San Francisco Jazz?

Or that from around the world would come fans and musicians to hear the Watters band and return home — whether to New Haven or Newcastle, Melbourne or Milan — as dedicated disciples spreading the gospel according to Lu, Turk and the band.

The Watters 1941-42 recordings had found their way around the globe by war's end. Combined with an astonishing renaissance of enthusiasm for early jazz and blues styles (particularly of the New Orleans-Chicago black community) and with large reissue programs by the major record companies an international trad jazz movement was underway.

Bebop, flourishing in the New York area by the end of the 40s, seemed incomprehensible and hostile to most mainstream swing and jazz fans; and bebop wasn't dance music, either.

The Watters Band, with a couple of dozen post-war recordings in circulation, regular radio shows and its own co-op nightclub ("Hambone Kelly's") was riding high by 1947-48.

Many in its complement had played with some of the old New Orleans musicians (Ory, Bunk Johnson, Mutt Carey, etc.) along the way and Watters, Murphy and Helm had written considerable new material for the band.

Rose had unearthed vintage ragtime and early jazz piano specialties — and second trumpeter Bob Scobey (playing "Louis Armstrong" to Watters' "King Oliver") was recording his variations on the San Francisco style under his own name with various members of the Bay Area's jazz community, including singer Clancy Hayes, who both Bing Crosby and Hoagy Carmichael felt was the best in the business.

And this was the period in which, as authors regularly note, "There was no jazz in San Francisco!"

There was so much, in fact, that full documentation is impossible.

The Yerba Buena Band gradually disintegrated. Hambone Kelly's closed in January of 1950, re-opened as "Alexander's," featuring owner Bob Scobey's band, then folded for good by the end of the year. The location is now a branch bank set in the El Cerrito Shopping Center, twenty-five minutes across the Bay Bridge from the Dawn Club site.

A brass plaque commemorating the Dawn's role in jazz history was installed, then removed; Annie Street was renamed Mark Twain Place, then named Annie Street again. Nothing commemorates Hambone Kelly's — other than the memories of thousands of San Francisco jazz fans.

The trad jazz movement continued to gain stature in the 50's. Scobey's and Murphy's bands (both containing Yerba Buena Band alums) performed steadily throughout the area with an increasing number of other Bay Area trad jazz bands playing and recording.

Scobey, with Hayes, clarinetist Bill Napier, trombonist Jack Buck, pianist Tiny Crump and others had a weekly television show; Jimmy Lyons' Saturday night radio broadcasts from the Club Hangover began in 1953.

The Frisco Jazz Band, Bay City Jazz Band, Burt Bales groups, and others were prominent on the scene.

Ory's Band with Carey spent much of its time in the Bay Area, Chicago cornetist Marty Marsala led a number of Bay Area-based groups; the George Lewis band from New Orleans played S.F.'s Club Hangover in 1953 (Jack Sheedy's band had opened the saloon a couple of years earlier) and clubs featuring San Francisco jazz came and went.

Papa Celestin's New Orleans band, Sidney Bechet, James P. Johnson, the Louis Armstrong All Stars (Earl Hines, Jack Teagarden and Barney Bigard among them) came through along the way— amazed by the crowds their older jazz styles attracted.

As the 1950s waned, the San Francisco Jazz title had become most closely associated with Turk Murphy who had travelled the land a bit by then and had enjoyed a number of years with a Columbia Records contract, thanks in large measure to record producer and San Francisco Jazz enthusiast George Avakian.

Murphy and the Earthquake McGoon's Club became living and lively San Francisco legends.

Watters, in his 40s, had long since left the music scene and moved to a rural homesite in Sonoma County. But dedicated fans and musicians regularly made the pilgrimage to his place, there to get advice, talk trad jazz, discuss records, drink wine and (increasingly) get scores from the Yerba Buena Band's book.

Pianist Pete Clute had replaced Rose in Murphy's band by now; Bill Bardin and Bob Mielke (trombonists), George Probert, clarinet-soprano sax, and a couple of dozen other younger musicians were playing prominent roles in Bay Area bands.

What a grand and glorious happening it all was; and is.

After all, the enthusiasm the Watters bandsmen and their early followers had for traditional jazz spread throughout the land and generated enclaves of new enthusiasts wherever it went.

Now, over fifty years after I first succumbed to the mesmerizing sounds of the Yerba Buena Jazz Band there are hundreds of trad jazz and/or Dixieland bands around the world—most of them loosely affiliated with astonishingly active jazz societies and festivals.

The annual Sacramento Jazz Jubilee, now twenty years old, features over 100 bands, a large proportion of them on-going pro-

above

Hot Music Society session at the Dawn Club, 1940. Bass, Vernon Alley, piano, Ernie Lewis, alto, Jerome Richardson, tenor, Bob Barfield, guitar, Benny Sexton, and trumpet, George "Cuz" Fleming. Photo courtesy of Maria Haas.

fessionals, young and old, from a dozen countries.

In their repertoires are stomps and struts; blues, rags, good-time songs, fox-trots; marches, spirituals and dirges. And compositions by Morton, Oliver, Armstrong—and Watters, Murphy, Helm, Hayes. As well as an increasing number of original scores, written in the real and righteous San Francisco Jazz manner.

Such is the legacy of the San Francisco Jazz style of the late 1940s — the music that the modern jazz critics and historians say didn't exist.

above

Interior Big Bear Tavern l-r: Wally Rose, Clancy Hayes (under the hat) Turk Murphy, Lu Watters, Bill Dart, Bob Scobey, Ellis Horne. Photo from the collection of Ed Lawless. Photographer unknown.

CHAPTER 1

THE 30s AND BEFORE: THE BIRTH, DEATH AND REVIVAL OF EARLY JAZZ

It is hard to imagine anyone, reflecting on the 1930s, to summarize the decade as the "good old days." Somewhere in the neighborhood of 25% of the work force was unemployed. Millions did not vote because they were going from city to city looking for work and therefore did not meet residency requirements. Still others could not afford to pay the poll tax imposed by many states as wages dropped over sixty percent. Needless to say millions of people stayed home, and those who could afford a radio listened to it. About 14 million families had a radio and this created jobs for musicians. By the end of the 30s the entire country was listening to swing music and jazz just wasn't to be heard. Jazz musicians were forced to find employment in swing bands and played the same numbers the same way every night.

While the San Francisco music scene was not devoid of jazz musicians and aspiring rehearsal groups at the time, there were few venues that supported any full time employment. Although at one time the top jobs were staff radio, theater pit, stage and movie recording soundtracks, by the late 30s those jobs were gone. Most radio staffs were in the process of moving to Hollywood and New York City; the cruise ships employing musicians had cut their schedules due to the depression; and many of the traveling shows on theater circuits such as the Orpheum, Fanchon and Marco, Pantages, and Fox had also cut back. Jazz clarinetist Bob Helm of Lu Watters' Yerba Buena Jazz Band says by 1937 things had become so bad that the San Francisco musicians Local Six hiring hall "bore a resemblance to a Roman arena...the gladiator cats with axes contesting for gigs as a band leader entered."

For musicians looking for casual employment or transfer members restricted from regular work, the Union at 230 Jones St. required a daily visit, and many members chose to live nearby in the uptown tenderloin bounded by Market, Larkin, O'Farrell and Mason Streets. Regular brothers came for social reasons: to play cards, shoot pool, dice and exchange information while waiting for a job call. At a glance, the reality of their situation was not immediately discernible. Even if their instruments were in hock, this cast of characters were particularly careful to hide their personal economic conditions behind their attire.

In clubs, the standard repertoire was a required mix of top 40, tangos, rumbas, waltzes and polkas, along with floor show back-ups. The hotels, for the most part, had succumbed to the three snoring tenor saxophones, one muted trumpet, flyswatter drums and double octave ascending piano scales formula. Some of the ballrooms and clubs also adopted this form. Rarely was a trombone employed. Tubas were relegated to Labor Day parades and Golden Gate Park. Banjos were the untouchables. Dance halls usually employed house bands and featured traveling headliners.

Freedom from all these stylized musical hang-ups was found in the neighborhood clubs. The dime jigs in Oakland were among the most interesting, where thirty to forty tunes—mostly head and ear arrangements—were played every hour. The Musicians Union Club also ran after hours and was a place for jazz players to get a drink, cash their check and sit in. These sessions were not so much a place to let off steam after an uninspiring gig; often they were a showcase for listening to performers of various musical tastes.

Among the other after-hour places was a spot located in a canyon over the ridge in the Oakland hills. Big Bear Tavern was so remote that finding it required an intimate knowledge of the East Bay, and only the dedicated chose to go there. Hughie, the owner, would close the doors to the public after 2 a.m., when he'd throw a private party and serve barbecue. He and his wife stayed up for the all night sessions that would eventually inspire the foundation of the Yerba Buena Jazz Band. In the words of clarinetist Bob Helm, "the band evolved out of boredom with jam session chestnuts and a routine of endless choruses into playing tunes with verses and multi-strained tunes. This was not so much a departure from current session procedures. It was a return to a more interesting period of popular music."

Although San Francisco certainly could not lay claim to being the birthplace of jazz, in his book *The Barbary Coast,* Herbert Asbury indicates that there was a lot of ragtime music activity going on around here prior to 1911. The dances mostly get the credit as originating here, for example—tunes like *Ballin' the Jack, Turkey Trot, Texas Tommy, Bunny Hug, Grizzly Bear, Castle House Strut.* Some of the all time great piano players performed on the Barbary Coast, including Mike Bernard, Lucky Roberts, Eubie Blake, Jelly Roll Morton and locals Sid La Protti and Alameda Levy.

Pianist La Protti had been a Barbary Coast legend from 1906 to 1921, when the city closed down that wild and wanton district. He met Morton in 1916 in Los Angeles where Jelly played at a hotel. Morton "for some reason or another, took a likin' to me," La Protti is quoted as saying in another book, *Jazz on the Barbary Coast* by Tom Stoddard. Morton gave La Protti a song to perform, *The Crave,* that became a big hit.

Morton got steamed, says La Protti. "Hey, a man lend you a number and you try to steal his stuff," said Morton, a mercurial genius who claimed to have invented jazz in 1901. Later Morton came to San Francisco and opened a club on Columbus.

"I'm going to close you down," boasted Morton to La Protti. and threatened to hire all his musicians away from him. Jelly ran into trouble a few months later when he fired his Colt .45 in the air during a brawl at his club. San Francisco's finest leaned hard on him to leave town and shortly thereafter he did just that, never to return to the city.

Alameda Levy was a regular at the Musicians Union club, a sharp pinochle player by reputation and a celebrity, appearing in Robert Ripley's *Oddities* as the World's Fastest Piano Player. At the union club he was continually prevailed upon to play his fastest (more notes per second), which included use of elbows, forearms, wrists and fingers. He would follow this rendition with a pop tune called *Dipsy Doodle*, using his own ten part harmony, which he always tried to demonstrate for Duke Ellington whenever he came to town.

Alameda was also a direct source of stories about the Barbary Coast era, and sometimes he would demonstrate a little ragtime, but that was about all there was to go on. In the late thirties the Musicians Local Unions were segregated and there was general apathy about jazz origins. Much of the early jazz had been trashed and the recording companies were not speculating on reissues with such limited potential. Charles Delauney had not yet compiled his discography and neither had Orrin

left

Sketch of Big Bear Tavern by Bud Luckey based on a rough sketch by Bob Helm.

Blackstone. Among the fans, musicians and record collectors, there was very limited information outside of the recorded music in private collections.

Occasionally information about background could be found in tabloid type magazines; *Variety* was mostly about show biz, but *Down Beat* and *Metronome* were popular sources. The British and foreign magazines such as *Melody Maker* along with writer Hugues Panassie were very informative, as well. To many musicians, however, the music and abilities of legendary players was just folklore described by somewhat eccentric enthusiasts. In the end, these enthusiasts prevailed enough to get together record sessions, jam sessions, and rehearsals playing from sketches or by ear from repeated listening to recordings. This sparked an interest in a quest for the obscure that was only hinted at by hearing the few available performances on usually very beat up discs. This was happening in the rehearsal rooms available in music stores in the Local Six vicinity—Rowlands, Union Music, and Hornung Piano Factory. Pat Patton was one of the early owners of a portable disc recorder which he occasionally brought up to these sessions. This did a lot to further interest in ensemble part playing instead of the popular riff background accompaniment employed in the jam sessions.

Verses were an integral part of the music as well as the lyrics. Playing an instrumental rouser like *Tiger Rag* without its first strain *Get Your Partner* quadrille would have been an affront to the dance audience of the 20s. Multi-strained compositions were the most difficult to learn, since many players had difficulty with the routines of *Royal Garden* and *Jazz Me Blues*. Some of the Original Dixieland Jazz Band music was familiar, but King Oliver and Jelly Roll Morton were still folklore figures.

Meanwhile, the bread and butter situation was the same. Not many of the frequenters of the Big Bear Tavern played in the same bands and those bands were not always very jazzy. The more interesting of the ballroom bands had many special charts, but still used mostly cut-up stocks of the current pops, since many of them had a short term life span.

Things started to heat up fast when Lu Watters put together an eleven piece band in 1938, a group Bob Helm would eventually call "the greatest ballroom band" that he ever played in. They got a booking in Sweet's Ballroom in Oakland, but because of Lu's repertoire, a long engagement was not considered likely.

Lu's use of obscure, out-of-date music associated with black bands rather than top 40s and current swing bands instrumentals was heavily attacked. Despite the criticism by other musicians, however, the band set an all-time attendance record at Sweet's which had only been topped once, by Ted Lewis. Still, the end of the Sweet's engagement marked the end of the Watters big band.

Members went on to different jobs. The 1939 World's Fair was opening and the music employment situation was improving as a result. Charlie Low opened his Forbidden City nightclub and employed a jazz band. Several hotels followed the Mark Hopkins in busting up the snoring with Bob Crosby's Big Band. Jack Joy's staff band at Treasure Island, the site of the World's Fair, began featuring Lu Watters on their daily radio program. The same year also marked the first appearance of the Yerba Buena Jazz Band at a Hot Jazz Club meeting at the Dawn Club.

The original band consisted of Lu, Turk, Bob Helm, Paul Lingle, Pat Patton, Bill Dart, and Squire Girsback. It had been rehearsing in the penthouse of the Mark Twain Hotel, but had not played any dates because of conflicting employment obligations.

For its first appearance at the Dawn Club, Bob Scobey filled in on a two-trumpet front line, but that turned out to be only a one-nighter. Frank Hunter, who ran the club, was impressed with the turnout and publicity and offered a regular couple of nights a week. This was agreeable to some members, but others could get more nights on other jobs. Making a living playing music was precarious. Putting together a band with a speculative future without a bankrolling agent was almost impossible. Eventually, however, with outside band jobs, personnel substitutions and an increase in scheduled nights, the regular band at the Dawn Club was established. The pianist was now Wally Rose who had worked on and off with Lu. Lu liked Wally because he was a fantastic sight reader and considered him to be one of the foremost ragtime players in the country.

left

The great King Oliver Band influenced Lu Watters. Shown standing is Louis Armstrong with Joseph "King" Oliver. Other inspirations in that band were Johnny Dodds and Edward "Kid" Ory to name just two. In 1920 Paul Lingle used to hear King Oliver's Band at the Pagoda Ballroom on Market Street in San Francisco. Louis Armstrong influenced Bob Scobey even more than Oliver.

above

Scott Joplin.
Paul Lingle and the others actively looked for sheet music of Scott Joplin's ragtime tunes. When Lu Watters band performed they generally included a ragtime number when few bands were playing this type of music. Later the movie *The Sting* did much to bring Joplin's music to the attention of the public. Both photographs were the gift of Turk Murphy.

right

Two singers who thrilled the musicians were "Ma" Rainey and Bessie Smith. Their early recordings reflected a direct blues style that appealed to the groups so they collected Paramount recordings by "Ma" Rainey (real name: Gertrude) and Columbia labels for Bessie Smith. Bessie really set the standard for other singers to follow.

left

They also listened to Thomas "Fats" Waller who combined humor with his playing. The authors could not resist using the boogie woogie folio pictured here because Fats hated this form of the blues and had a clause in his engagement contracts that he would NOT play boogie woogie.

above

Sheet music was collected by the members of the Yerba Buena Jazz Band. Here are a few examples.

top

Jelly Roll Morton and his Red Hot Peppers. l-r: Andrew Hilaire, Kid Ory, George Mitchell, John Lindsay, Morton, Johnny St. Cyr, and Omer Simeon (partially visible).

above

Jelly Roll Morton's calling card. From the collection of Charles Campbell.

right

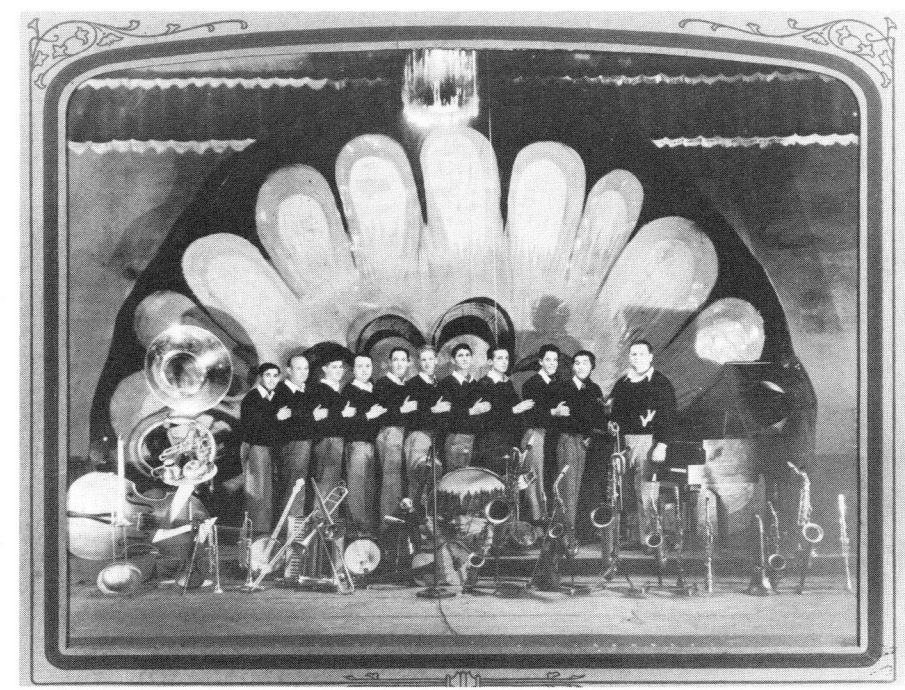

Fritz Wolcott's Valley Vagabonds, the bandstand of the Merry Garden Ballroom, circa 1932. From left: Joe Shimon, drums - later had his own band and joined his father's business. Eddie Bettencourt, trumpet, trombone and tuba, formed his own band and was a ranch foreman. Buddy Wolter, trombone - still active in music and is a long time Musician's Union representative living in Stockton, California. Cesare Graziano, banjo, guitar, trombone, accordion and arrangements - became associate of Guido Diero and accordion schools, a teacher in San Francisco's Mission District. Bob Helm, reeds, arrangements, vocals - Modesto Junior College music major, still active in music in Larkspur, California. Jimmy Lewis, trumpet, vocals, arrangements – Modesto Junior College music major, music teacher King City, California. Frank Marks, reeds, arrangements - College of the Pacific music major, teacher and part time musician Napa, California. Frank Willis, strings, bass, guitar, vocals - teacher Santa Cruz, California. Vernon (Barney) DeSylva - piano, arrangements - joined Uncle Buddy's Song Writer's staff in Hollywood, later on staff College of the Pacific, Stockton, California. Frank O'Neal, vocals - continued as vocalist part time in Merced, California. Fred Wolcott, leader, violin reeds - graduate of the College of the Pacific, Stockton, California as a music major and arranger - retired from music to manage the family ranch in Livingston, California.

Bob Helm recalls: Our tour had included many break-jump one-nighters again on the return to the West Coast and a longer promised engagement at the Venice Ballroom in the Los Angeles area. However, the agent had miscalculated by getting the band too close to home. The Salt Lake City Ballroom engagement concluded; the group jumped in the bus and drove non-stop West. Somehow the "stick together and go to the top" esprit de corps credo had lost its credibility and a big cheer went up at the sight of the California state line sign and several members got out and kissed the ground at the Inspection Station. As the tired old GMC compression chamber rolled down highway 99 each cat debarked at his respective valley town and some I've never seen or heard about to this day some fifty-eight years later.

right

The Bert Trejue Band at the Willows in Reno. (l-r) Duke Eyselee, Bill Ames, Bert Trejue, Phil Bodley, Dude Nix and Jack Crook. Jack later worked with the Capital City Jazz Band, Frisco Jazz Band, Turk Murphy and Bob Scobey.

left

Vernon Alley shown here playing bass with a small dance band. l–r; Wesley Peoples, Vernon, Jake Porter and Vernon's brother Eddie Alley. For purposes of economy, many touring bands hired local musicians rather then travel with a full band. Vernon played with just about every band because in addition to being a gifted musician, he was—and is— dependable.

left

The Merle Howard Orchestra at the Cal Neva Lodge August 28, 1939. l-r: Byron Berry, Turk Murphy, Morely Gale, Cliff Davis, Mike McDaniel, Ed Litten, Raynor Guy, Dan Forster, Bud Congdon and Merle Howard. When Lu Watters, Pat Patton Turk Murphy, Paul Lingle and Bob Helm would get together after hours they all agreed that their jobs were boring and they found enjoyment playing and talking about New Orleans style jazz.

right

In 1933 Russ Bennett won a contest resulting in a singing spot with Herbie Field's Orchestra, the house band at the Mark Hopkins Hotel in San Francisco. Russ could not remember the name of the man on the left (he came in second). Russ is in the middle and the woman is the band's female singer, Dorothy Lamour, who went on to great fame in Hollywood.

left

Cover of souvenir book for the 1939 World's Fair at Treasure Island, California. The Fair was a magnet for musicians and there were many playing jobs available.

right

The Sweet's Ballroom house band in 1939 which played tangos, fox trots and some jazz. (l-r) Back row: Squire Girsback, Gordon "Gramps" Edwards, Bob Scobey, Lu Watters, Bill Yeaman and Hiram "Hi" Gates. Front Row: Russ Bennett, Bob Helm, Henry Abrahamson and Ken "Buss" Greene. Not shown is the piano player who was usually Dave Olson. Subs on piano were Paul Lingle or Ray Jahnigen. The front man in the top hat was Harold Atwood.

right

The Dawn Club was located at 20 Annie Street in San Francisco, an alley-sized street that runs from Market to Mission Street. The club was right behind the Palace Hotel, in the basement of the Monadnock Building.

far right

One of the first to greet you was Augie Giretto who collected a cover charge of 50 cents. Here he is shown at the bar with Lu Watters. Augie acted as the business manager for the YBJB and performed various duties. By the way, Lu's first name was Lucius.

CHAPTER 2

THE 40S THE REVIVAL THRIVES

Charles Campbell took the long way around to reach San Francisco's jazz scene in the 1940s. He went by way of China. Campbell fell in love with jazz in the early 1930s as a student in Shanghai. He lived there with his parents in its thriving, jiving community of European and American expatriates who played out the end of a lost era even as Imperial Japan prepared for its soon-to-be-launched war of conquest against China. Campbell, a fourth-generation Californian, was in Shanghai because of his father's gold fever. His father had operated a gold mine in Siberia years earlier, but had been detained, then run out when the Bolsheviks took over in 1917. "He had some deals in China," says Campbell, "but he really went to Shanghai to get closer to all that gold he still remembered in Siberia."

In this exotic milieu, young Campbell met Teddy Weatherford, an old time jazz legend who had played with Louis Armstrong in New Orleans but then had vanished from the Big Easy. Trouble with the law, it was rumored. Weatherford and his band played in a supper club at the dog track in Shanghai, and they were the toast of the town's foreign and Chinese elite. Campbell scored big with his fellow students when he hired Weatherford and his band to play one of his school's events.

With World War II beginning, the Campbells left China for Los Angeles. Charles became a connoisseur of old jazz records—-King Oliver, Louis Armstrong, Jelly Roll Morton. "By then jazz was history," Campbell recalls. At least that is what he thought until he made a trip to San Francisco in 1941 and walked into the Dawn Club. "I heard Watters and the band playing *Come Back Sweet Papa*," he says. "I thought I'd died and gone to heaven!"

Campbell became a regular on the scene. He moved to San Francisco and opened an art supply store, later a gallery. Eventually he started and ran one of the best jazz joints ever, the Italian Village in North Beach. That's where a 15-year-old named Peter Clute used to slip in unobtrusively to listen to Wally Rose and all the rest of those who already were becoming jazz legends in their own rights. But that's another story.

The trad jazz revival didn't exactly sail smoothly through the 1940s. When the Yerba Buena Jazz Band opened at the Dawn Club, the audiences were enthusiastic about the music but didn't know the names of most of the tunes. In order to help alleviate this problem, a printed program of the nightly sets was passed out at the door. This chamber music recital approach helped immeasurably in re-introducing the titles and included composer credits.

Nevertheless, some old friends and officials of the Musicians Union tried to discourage members from throwing away their careers performing dated and unpopular black music. But none of this discouraged the musicians.

Neither were fans discouraged, or weaned away by the ubiquitous, popular swing music that permeated the 1940s. Maria Haas remembers riding busses and streetcars to come listen, along with a lively and growing army of fans, many of whom liked both swing and trad jazz. "I liked Benny Goodman," admits Haas, "But I drew the line at Glenn Miller."

Despite its initial success, the Yerba Buena Jazz Band at the Dawn Club was having rhythm and dynamics problems. The slow tunes slowed with the soft and the fast tunes increased tempo with the loud. This made some of the front line fight to keep kick-off tempo and as a result, the dynamics suffered. The boiling point was finally reached in 1940 on a Saturday night with Turk Murphy giving notice and stomping off.

Sunday, Turk called Bob Helm to check out a rehearsal Monday at Frank O'Mea's house in the San Francisco's Sunset district. When things finally shook out, Ellis Horne took over for Bob and Hi Gates replaced Turk. It would take six years for the original group to get back together again.

With all this going on, another complication arrived with the BMI/ASCAP wars about performance pay. BMI boycotted ASCAP and refused to play any of their music on the radio. Air time music thereafter consisted of public domain music. Stephen Foster's *Jeannie with the Light Brown Hair* became a hit. Meanwhile, BMI's hired staff of songwriters were grinding tunes out twenty-four hours a day. As a result of this conflict, many clubs who had been paying ASCAP monthly followed suit. It was a lively time for tune sleuths checking the juke boxes and clubs suspected of sneaking in ASCAP music. Eventually the American Federation of Musicians was able to resolve the differences although not to all the members' satisfaction.

The popularity of the Yerba Buena Jazz Band was helped by the radio live broadcasts and when the band's first recordings became available. Not everybody was enthusiastic, of course. The press and the previewers had mixed feelings about the music, much the same as those expressed by the band's formerly mentioned colleagues. The adjective "revival" was not used in the early descriptions, but came later. Some uninitiated scribes even used the categorical term "new music" to describe the sound.

But none of these complications mattered much compared to the biggest thing on every one's mind then—-the war. Unfortunately, while the reputation of the YBJB and the San Francisco style was growing, this period in 1941 was a time of apprehension about the members service related availability. One way to keep playing would have been to follow the example of Glenn Miller and the others who were able to join the service as a band and stay together. Turk Murphy tried to arrange for the band to join the Navy as a group. This opportunity was presented when a recruiting officer from the Alameda Naval Air Station showed up one day. Some members enlisted. Murphy himself joined the Navy. But pulling the group together under a Navy banner never worked out. Some members joined other services; scattering to fight for their country rather than just play for it.

Throughout the war, the Dawn Club continued its jazz policy with a group of players which included Benny Strickler and that carried on with a YBJB repertorial program. This band gradually changed as members went into the service or left for more lucrative employment as nights at the club were cut back.

It wasn't until 1946 that the original YBJB with Lu Watters, Turk Murphy and Bob Helm was revived, but the post war band was to start out with a musical perception of its previous repertoire that reached a new high. It seemed as though everyone had assimilated the repertoire in retrospect during the war years. The new/old YBJB again opened at the Dawn Club to an enthusiastic, though somewhat differently jazz-oriented audience.

The programmed tunes list again was handed out at the door. The numbers were announced and

left

Early 1940s photo of an informal gathering with l-r: Turk Murphy, Willie Thorpe, Bob Helm.

there was dancing as usual, with air shots again. The West Coast recording sessions started and there were outside dates to play. The recording for the West Coast label was done on the Dawn Club off days for several months.

The choice of Avalon Ballroom's bandstand was made because of its live acoustical characteristics, but the choice made it necessary to transmit the mike signals by telephone to Photo and Sound studio on Montgomery Street across from the Palace Hotel. This involved using a Sutter and Van Ness phone line over several miles of questionable high-signal carrying cables. Although this was not a party line, various glitches appeared on Photo and Sound master acetates and the takes had to be re-done. The bandstand mikes also picked up incoming rings from the ballroom pay phones until the bells were stuffed for each recording date.

The original schedule was to try for a half-dozen tunes each session, however, this plan became quite variable with the above headaches added on top of basic problems such as getting comfortable with the repertoire and introducing new music. Moreover, when the first West Coast 78 RPMS were issued, the shellac was of poor quality because of wartime availability. As a result, these discs turned gray after a few plays and became pitted after a few more. It wasn't until Nesuhi Ertegan had spent a hectic year re-mastering these for LP albums—*The San Francisco Style*—that the sound was stabilized and improved.

These technical production problems were followed by pressing financial problems for the band. Attendance at the Dawn Club was off, but not enough to warrant a move. Meanwhile, the partnership of which Lu Watters and Bob Scobey were founding members had been turned over to the Club's management during their service period. As a result, the IRS had not been paid and the money had been used by the operators for other purposes. While the government was willing to carry the back tax debt with pay-back installments, the partnership opted for Chapter 11 and dissolved. New Year's Eve 1946 marked the last of the Yerba Buena Jazz Band's appearances at Annie Street.

There were several job offers by booking agents, night clubs and the Fairmont Hotel, but it was felt that the music's integrity would suffer and concessions to the top 40 requests that had been all but eliminated from the repertoire would be again pressured into the venue. Instead, the band decided to open their own club.

Several spots were considered. Some did not have the capacity, others lacked the right location. Sally Rand's Hollywood Club in El Cerrito in the East Bay, which had closed during the war, was finally chosen. At first, this seemed an appalling choice to San Franciscans and Peninsula fans. Questions arose such as: Where *is* El Cerrito? How on earth do you *get* there? Do you really expect enough people to come support a full eight-piece group? It's a two-hour excursion to that place via public transportation! And on and on...

But there was an upside to El Cerrito, which was known as the "strip" along San Pablo Avenue. There were a dozen clubs operating in the vicinity. Some featured headline shows and most had music, dining and dancing. Some also featured 24-hour gambling, off-track betting, slot machines, and high stakes games. All of this Las Vegas type activity was good for everyone. Instead of creating a highly competitive atmosphere, each place had something to offer. Club hopping was the big draw and the clubs encouraged it by bringing large parties to each other's establishments. The 204 San Pablo location was across from an old established club, the Kona. Next door was the Rancho San Pablo, and down the street were the It Club, the Wagon Wheel and the Six Belles. A little bit south you could find the Albany, and there were numerous others.

Other big plusses nearby were the campuses of U.C. Berkeley and the California College of Arts and Crafts. The El Cerrito Dog Racing Track was over the back parking lot fence and Golden Gate Fields horse racing track was over the hill in Albany.

Arrangements for the liquor license and lease were secured and the opening date was set. Renovations, stocking of the bar and kitchen, constructing a dance floor, hiring of staff, creating the band-

left

This song title card was given out at the Dawn Club because it helped those who did not know the titles. It also made a nice souvenir.

stand, publicity and selecting a name all took time.

Of the names suggested, one offered by Lu was chosen as most representative. Hambone Kelly, an acquaintance of Lu's and a performer from the earlier minstrel days was honored. In the tradition of a minstrel show, one of the line was introduced as Mr. Hambone. He acknowledged his introduction, bowed, and went into a short body-slapping, finger-popping, hollow-jaw thumping and rhythmic tap-dance routine. Since there were no publicity shots and Hambone's whereabouts unknown, some answers to curious queries had to be resolved. There was at that time a popular painting around known as *The Gay Philosopher* by Major whose subject was a smiling, bearded, string-tied, frock-coated individual of obvious barroom demeanor. This was displayed as Hambone. Lu's dance piece *Doin' the Hambone* provided breaks for the performers to carry out their minstrel improvisations.

Hambone Kelly's had two openings: the first trial shakedown operation was more for friends and acquaintances who had donated so much of their time and financial support. The club was very successful with long lines outside waiting to enter on the weekends. The appearance of the Yerba Buena Jazz Band on Rudy Blesh's *This Is Jazz* program broadcast nationally was a good boost for attendance and the West Coast recordings were receiving publicity internationally.

After a year of this apparently successful operation, it was hoped that enough of the original loans would be paid off that the band could start drawing more than the union minimum wage. However, this salary increase never took place. Hambone Kelly's Inc. was formed of most of the band members, but its monthly financial statements had never included a

right

Another flyer advertising the YBJB.

profit and loss operating report. The complexities involved, seemingly were insurmountable. In the end, this led to the break up of the band. Some of the corporation members eventually withdrew their investments and headed for other employment with a brighter monetary future.

And there was another big blow to the band: Lu Watters had been suffering with a double hernia. Blowing trumpet had become excruciatingly painful and surgery became necessary. This put him out for several months. Bob Scobey left to form his own band, and Turk Murphy soon did likewise. Wally Rose, Bill Dart, and Harry Mordecai obtained other employment as the nights had been cut, resulting in an impossible living salary.

In desperation, Lu proposed that the club start a policy of dollar dinners to attract neighborhood diners and also started showing old-time movies from 6-8 p.m. Harry Mordecai was often the projectionist. He also opened three nights a week and Sunday afternoons with other featured groups when available. This created much extra duty, but enabled Hambone's to last a little longer. By mid 1950, Rose and Dart rejoined the reduced five piece YBJB which, in Lu's own words, "went down the tubes" on New Year's Eve along with Hambone Kelly's in 1951.

Still, the jazz revival in the Bay Area supported at least eight full-time employed groups, each with their own varied repertoires of early and sometimes pop music. The ones on the El Cerrito strip and vicinity suffered from the incorporation into Richmond of the former free-wheeling territory. With the new city ordinances, it ceased to be an attraction and many of the old as well as new clubs went belly-up along with Hambone Kelly's.

top left

On the Dawn Club band stand are l-r: Lu Watters, Bob Scobey, Turk Murphy, Bob Helm and Wally Rose.

bottom left

The first sides for Jazz Man Records were recorded in December 1941. Shown here are l-r: Turk Murphy, Squire Girsback, Lu Watters, Clancy Hayes, Bob Scobey, Bill Dart, Russ Bennett, Wally Rose and Ellis Horne. The two in the booth are "Biff" Leonetti - roommate of Augie Giretto - and Dave Stuart of Jazz Man Records.

above

After the success of the first YBJB sides the Jazz Man label released four sides by Jelly Roll Morton. In addition they recorded Bunk Johnson, Kid Ory and Johnny Wittwer among others. Brothers Ahmet and Nesuhi Ertegun were the owners of the Jazz Man label (which was started by Marili and Dave Stuart. Marili later married Nesuhi) and deserve much credit for the traditional jazz revival. Later they sold their company to Les Koenig of Good Time Records.

below

Photo of Benny Strickler on horn. (l-r) Lou "Pappy" Vann and Joe Blackburn, 1942-43. Benny was considered a good horn man so Russ Bennett encouraged him to replace Lu Watters and Bob Scobey when they joined the service. He recorded a few sides which were later released on the Good Time Jazz label. Russ regretted asking Benny to play as he soon became ill again. He suffered from tuberculosis. He later died in a sanitarium at only 29 years of age. He worked with Seger Ellis, Bob Wills and others.

above

Photo of Lu Watters and Turk Murphy with a Navy pick-up band.

inset

Opinions were mixed about the YBJB as you can tell by this headline on Herb Caen's column circa 1946. Some liked it, some didn't, but the crowds came.

above

Recording session for the Exner label circa 1945. l-r: Joe Darensbourg, Alton Redd, Montudi Garland, Kid Ory, Buster Wilson, Mutt Carey and Bud Scott.

right

This is Jazz booklet. *This is Jazz* was a series of jazz lectures given at the San Francisco Museum of Modern Art in 1943 by Rudi Blesh who was one of the earlier authors of jazz books (*Shining Trumpets* was one of his books). While Rudi got all the credit, Bill Colburn made a significant contribution to the program.

top left

Buster Wilson. Burt Bales once remarked how sad it was that Buster never recorded solo "as he was the closest to "Jelly Roll". Those of us who had the opportunity to listen to Buster would agree with Burt.

below

Kid Ory and Papa "Mutt" Carey. Ory's Creole Jazz Band recorded in the 1920s and were brought out of retirement because of the revival. They enjoyed great success. Photo courtesy of Charles Campbell.

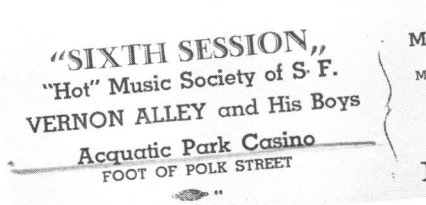

right

Some tickets to Hot Music Society concerts (Later known as Hot Jazz Society).

below

Peter Tamony's membership card. He was one of the real jazz fans and a founder of the Hot Music and Hot Jazz Societies. Peter also did considerable research in newspaper archives to find references to jazz in the early 1900's.

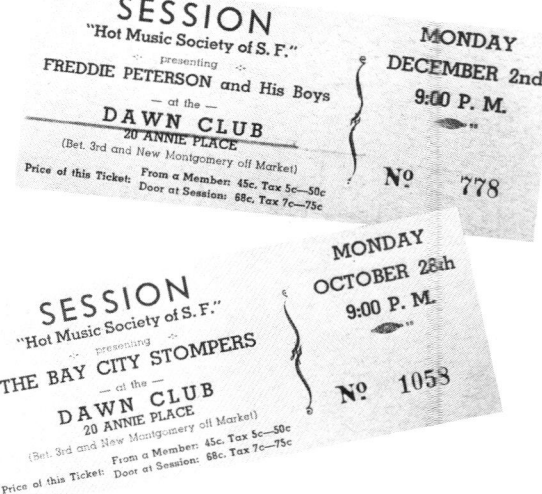

The Great Jazz Revival

below

Photo of Louis Armstrong with Bunk Johnson donated to the Jazz Foundation by Turk Murphy, who enjoyed telling the story about how some bands tried to emulate Bunk Johnson. They purchased Bunk's recordings and religiously copied his style even to the point of "laying out" (stop playing) on trumpet during the ensemble as Bunk occasionally would do. Turk explained that the "laying out" was done to give Bunk time to adjust the false teeth which gave him some difficulty! There are many conflicting stories as to just how Bunk was "rediscovered". He was working as a field hand in New Iberia, Louisiana and was just about toothless. We think it was a collaborative effort between people like Bill Russell, Bill Colburn and the YBJB. Members of the YBJB and fans like Charles Campbell sent donations to help Bunk purchase new teeth.

above

Hot Jazz Society of San Francisco flyer. The Hot Jazz Society of San Francisco was started by a group of record collectors who later had concerts of live jazz performances. The sponsors were an interesting mix of people. For example, Harry Bridges, the leader of the San Francisco longshoremen was a member.

top left

Bunk Johnson and the Hot Seven.

bottom left

Saunders King and his Orchestra. The two bands provided an interesting contrast of musical styles. Sister Lottie Peavay was a fabulous singer. It is too bad she never wanted to record commercially.

below

Jazz Versus Swing concert December 12, 1943.

The Great Jazz Revival

below

Jive at Eleven Five by The Saunders King Band was the theme for the Ted Lenz radio show which was very popular in the Bay Area, King's band had many fans and his recordings sold well. Saunders certainly deserves more recognition than he has been given.

above

The Ted Lenz radio show where jazz greats would put in guest appearances when in town. Shown are l-r: Bob Best, Louis Armstrong, Ted Lenz and Bunk Johnson. Bob was a frequent visitor to the Dawn Club and liked to sing with the band.

below

Article from Downbeat Magazine.

above

The YBJB rehearsed for several weeks before re-opening at the Dawn Club. Shown are l-r: Harry Mordecai, Turk Murphy, Lu Watters, Bill Dart, Bob Scobey, Bob Helm, Dick Lammi and Wally Rose. Notice the piano has been turned around for better communications at rehearsal.

right

Flyer announcing the return of the Yerba Buena Jazz Band to the Dawn Club on March 1, 1946. The San Francisco Fire Department closed the doors at 9 p.m. on opening night because they estimated there were 900 fans in the club. A long line of people had to be turned away.

The Great Jazz Revival

left

Folder containing a photo of the YBJB could be obtained at the Dawn Club.

above

Richard Donovan was the writer for the San Francisco Chronicle who first called the YBJB *The Minstrels of Annie Street* and inspired Turk to compose a tune with the same title.

right

Photo sold with folder. Members of the band are l-r: Harry Mordecai, Turk Murphy, Lu Watters, Bill Dart, Bob Scobey, Bob Helm, Wally Rose and Dick Lammi. Photo by Melgar Studios of San Francisco.

```
              LU WATTERS'
          YERBA BUENA JAZZ BAND
                    PLAYS
         THURSDAY, FRIDAY, SATURDAY AND SUNDAY
                      AT
              THE DAWN CLUB
              20 Annie Street, San Francisco


            P R O G R A M -- Friday November 1, 1946

        ( Washboard Willie . . . . . . . . . . . Turk Murphy
   1.   ( Beale Street Blues . . . . . . . . . . W. C. Handy
        ( Weary Blues. . . . . . . . . . . . . . Matthews

        ( Reunion Joys . . . . . . . . . . . . . Bob Helm
        ( Memphis Blues. . . . . . . . . . . . . W. C. Handy
   2.   ( Ace in the Hole. . . . . . . . . . . . traditional
        ( Hooking Cow Blues. . . . . . . . . . . Williams
        ( Ostrich Walk . . . . . . . . . . . . . La Rocca & Shields

        ( Auntie Skinners Chicken Dinners. . . . Morse
        ( Working Man Blues. . . . . . . . . . . King Oliver
   3.   ( You've Gotta See Mama Every Night. . . Conrad
        ( Pastime Rag. . . . . . . . . . . . . . Matthews
        ( Muskrat Ramble . . . . . . . . . . . . Kid Ory

        ( Down Home Rag. . . . . . . . . . . . . Sweatman
        ( Antigua Blues . . . . . . . . . . . . .Lu Watters
   4.   ( Sunburst Rag . . . . . . . . . . . . . James Scott
        ( Terrible Blues . . . . . . . . . . . . Richard M. Jones
        ( Trombone Rag . . . . . . . . . . . . . Turk Murphy

               BROADCAST (11:00 to 11:15
          on K.G.O. and other Stations of the A.B.C. Network)

        ( Friendless Blues . . . . . . . . . . . traditional
        ( Maple Leaf Rag . . . . . . . . . . . . Scott Joplin
   5.   ( New Orleans Stomp. . . . . . . . . . . Lil Hardin
        ( Harlem Rag . . . . . . . . . . . . . . Tom Turpin
        ( 1919 Rag . . . . . . . . . . . . . . . traditional

        ( Jazzin' Babies Blues . . . . . . . . . Richard M. Jones
        ( I'm Goin' Huntin'. . . . . . . . . . . Waller
   6.   ( Dying Gamblers Blues . . . . . . . . . traditional
        ( Emperor Norton's Hunch . . . . . . . . Lu Watters

        ( Sage Hen Strut . . . . . . . . . . . . Lu Watters
        ( The Cascades . . . . . . . . . . . . . Scott Joplin
   7.   ( Richard M. Jones Blues . . . . . . . . Richard M. Jones
        ( New Orleans Stomp. . . . . . . . . . . Hardin & Armstrong
        ( Friendless Blues . . . . . . . . . . . traditional

             LU WATTERS RECORDS ON SALE AT YOUR DEALERS

         West Coast 101                    West Coast 103
             Canal Street Blues                Trombone Rag
             Antigua Blues                     Sunburst Rag

         West Coast 102                    West Coast 104
             Chattanooga Stomp                 Big Bear Stomp
             Creole Belles                     Working Man Blues
```

left

Program sheets were given out each night and became collectors items as well as demonstrating the large music "book" of the YBJB.

above

While in a college art class in 1942, Leslie Rolfe did this water color of the YBJB. She has become a well-known artist and is still a jazz fan.

> *the jazz man*
> *presents*
> *the first Southern California*
> *appearance of*
>
> **LU WATTERS'**
> **YERBA BUENA JAZZ BAND**
>
> JAMES P. JOHNSON
>
> ALBERT NICHOLAS ZUTTY SINGLETON
>
> Wednesday 8:30 p.m.
> **JUNE 1**
>
> **PASADENA CIVIC AUDITORIUM**
> 300 E. GREEN STREET — PASADENA
> *tickets: 2.40—1.80—1.20 inc. Fed. Tax*
>
> **TICKETS NOW ON SALE**
> **AT JAZZ RECORD STORES**
> FOR INFORMATION CALL
> **HIllside 1588**
> NOON TO 8 P.M.

> # HUNGRY?
> RED BEANS AND RICE, CREOLE 50c
> ITALIAN SPAGHETTI WITH MEAT AND SAUCE 75c
> SCALLOPINI 90c
>
> These prices may surprise you, but they're in line with the Dawn Club's new policy of lowering your entertainment budget.
>
> # WANT TO DANCE?
> LU WATTERS' FAMOUS YERBA BUENA JAZZ BAND PLAYS SUNDAY EVENINGS 4 till 8:30 and every Wednesday, Thursday, Friday and Saturday nights 8:30 to 12:30
>
> *NO ADMISSION • NO MINIMUM*
> *AT ANY TIME*
>
> ### The DAWN CLUB
> **20 ANNIE STREET**
>
> JUST OFF MARKET STREET - BETWEEN THE PALACE HOTEL AND THE EXAMINER BLDG.

above left

Postcard flyer concerning the YBJB's first Southern California appearance on June 1, 1946.

above right

Flyer announcing a new price policy at the Dawn Club. Unfortunately it was not enough to overcome back income taxes which had not been paid during the war so the last night was New Year's Eve 1946.

left

Ad for Burt Bales. Note the ad referred to "Bert". He never recorded with Bunk Johnson for the Capitol Record Company. Burt said "That was some newspaper guy's idea." Burt and Bunk corresponded and Bunk often stayed at Burt's home when he wasn't playing or, in Burt's words, "...when he wasn't trying to locate all the cat houses in town."

below

Recording of *Canadian Capers* on the Good Time Jazz Label. Jack Fina —of *Bumble Boogie* fame— worked with Burt Bales to try to learn more of a "jazz feel" for his recordings. Subsequently he recorded *Canadian Capers* on the MGM label and it sold rather well. When Turk Murphy found out Burt was a little bit miffed about this he hired an actor to stand in front of the band stand one night repeatedly asking Burt to play *Canadian Capers*. After Burt finally played the tune the actor said "That's not *Canadian Capers*." Burt rather forcefully replied that it certainly was. The actor than said, well maybe it was, but Jack Fina plays it better! Burt almost came off the band stand, but everyone started laughing and he realized he had been set up.

left

Interior of the Yerba Buena Music Shop, which was located at 5721 Grove Street in Oakland. Behind the counter is Dick Oxtot. For many years this was a hang-out for musicians and jazz fans. Vivian and Ray were often on the radio and were extremely knowledgeable about jazz. Photo donated by Dick Oxtot. Notice the print of the Gay Philosopher on the wall.

right

Flyer announcing four new releases on the West Coast Label (the YBJB's own label). This flyer was mailed to customers of the Yerba Buena Music Shop, owned by Vivian and Ray Boarman. Their mailing list was always up-to-date.

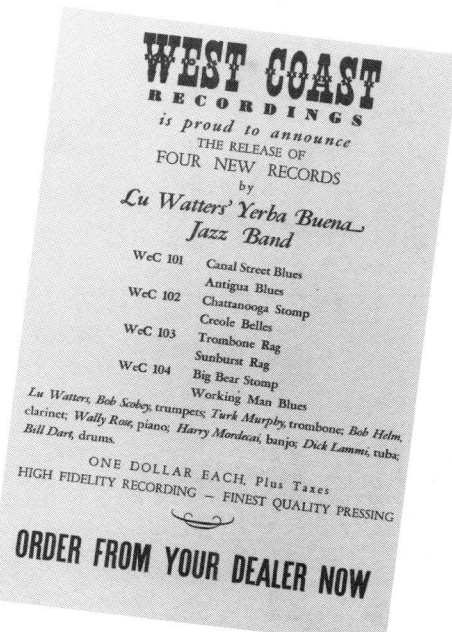

above

Photo of Frisco Jazz Band. L-r: Jack Buck (on valve trombone), Eddie Smith, Gordon "Grandpa" Edwards, and Jack Crook. Not shown are Russ Bennett, Ray Jahnigen and Pat Patton.

below

The Pacific Label issued quite a few sides recorded by The Frisco Jazz Band. One was a big hit, *A Huggin' and A Chalkin*. George Avakian, a well-known jazz fan who later became an A&R man for Columbia Records, wrote in his column *On Records*: "Clancy Hayes, composer of *A Huggin' and A Chalkin* sings the definitive version of his novelty hit with a virtually unknown group of west coast musicians, known as the Frisco Jazz Band, who makes up what appears to be the third-best jazz outfit in the country. The other two, oddly enough, also are in San Francisco: Kid Ory's Creole Band and Lu Watters' Yerba Buena Jazz Band."

above

Pat Patton, the organizer of The Frisco Jazz Band. He also worked on cruise ships and with Turk Murphy and Lu Watters.

above

Nighttime photo of Hambone Kelly's taken by Harry Mordecai.

below

Cartoon of Lu Watters serving a hambone. This also hung in the front bar. It was appropriate as Lu spent much of his time in the kitchen. This cartoon was done by Clark Wright who, along with some others, did the lettering of jazz tunes behind the front bar.

right

Daytime photo of Hambone's, also by Harry Mordecai.

Grand Opening

HAMBONE KELLY'S
204 San Pablo Ave. • El Cerrito

FRIDAY, JUNE 20

LU WATTERS'
YERBA BUENA JAZZ BAND

- Restaurant and Bar Opens at 5:00 P.M. Daily Except Mondays • Private Banquet Room for Club Parties • Good Food Served Family Style or A La Carte • A Jazz Band Plays Every Friday, Saturday and Sunday Night • 20-Minute Service on the "L" Bus from San Francisco • No admission or Cover Charge at Any Time • Free Parking • 350 Car Capacity

above

Opening night of Hambone's, June 20, 1947. l-r: Turk Murphy, Lu Watters, Harry Mordecai, Bob Scobey, Bob Helm, Dick Lammi and Bill Dart (partially visible). Photo by Tom Quinn. (Phil Elwood is on the right with his back to the camera). Lu Watters was dating Pat Joyce (who later became his wife) at this time. Pat's father was not sure he approved of Lu. He got into an altercation with him during which Lu was shot in the hand. Although Lu wasn't seriously hurt, the resulting headlines created a lot of publicity for the club and increased attendance. Lu and his father-in-law later became great friends.

below

Hambone Kelly's had front and back bars. This is a view of the wall behind the front bar showing the names of various jazz tunes. The trumpet was sent to Lu from Erfurt, Germany by Bob Helm. It was "liberated" from the Wehrmacht Band when Bob was with Patton's 80th Infantry.

above

Photo of the *Gay Philosopher* by Henry Major. Lu Watters thought that this painting caught the flavor of Hambone's.

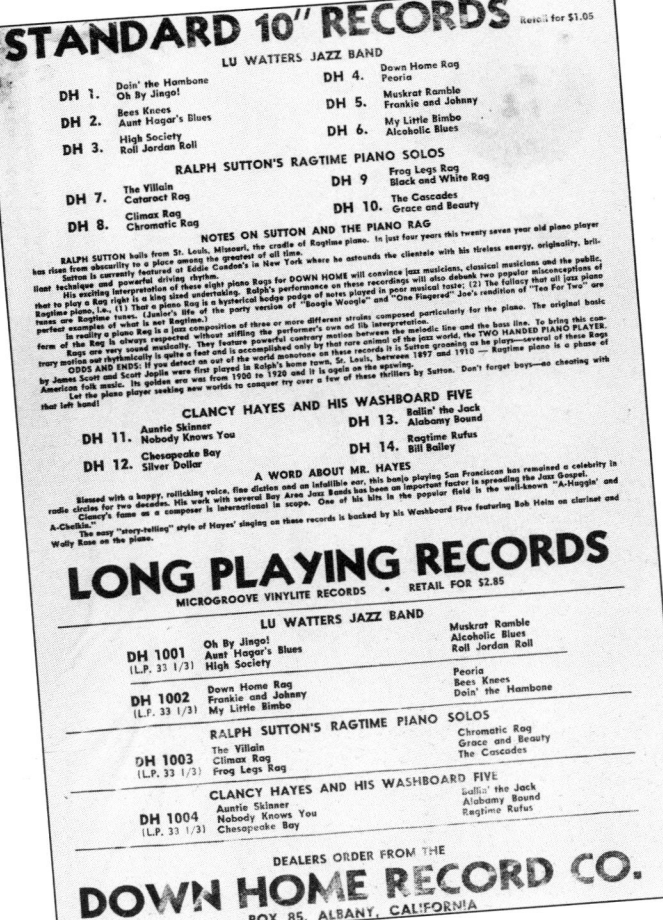

opposite

The very popular Wally Rose. Photograph by Al Rodriguez.

above

Two typical flyers that Lu used to promote record sales.

above

Some of those at the private Christmas party at Hambone's, 1947. Left: "Cookie", Ma Watters, Augie Giretto, Barbara Scobey, Bob Scobey. Right: Mrs Joyce (mother of Pat Watters), Lu Watters, Madeline Giretto, Turk Murphy. Photo taken by Harry Mordecai.

right

Lu's theme song - *Friendless Blues*.

below

The YBJB in the late 40s at Hambone's. l-r: Turk Murphy, Bill Dart, Lu Watters, Bob Scobey, Bob Helm, Harry Mordecai, Dick Lammi and Johnny Wittwer. Johnny recorded solo piano pieces for the Jazz Man and Stinson labels and with a trio for the Exner label. Dr. Exner was a jazz fan from Seattle who recorded Johnny and others.

above

Johnny Wittwer and Dick Lammi. (Yes, Virginia the YBJB did not always use a tuba!). Johnny Wittwer was with the YBJB, Turk Murphy, Wingy Manone and others. He generally worked as a soloist, and was a very good traditional jazz player as well as an exceptional boogie woogie player. Dick Lammi was one of the real characters of the YBJB and the band members enjoyed putting ash trays, etc. in his tuba. Once, when the band went early morning eel fishing Dick did not bother to change from his tux and could not understand why he should change.

below

Photo of Castle Jazz Band. They recorded in the Northwest on their own label. George Bruns, the trombonist, became a studio musician in Hollywood and achieved fame for composing the hit tune *Davy Crockett*. Some of the members joined the Turk Murphy Band. The excellent cornetist, Jim Goodwin, is Bob Goodwin's son. Photo by Ackroyd Photography in Portland.

above

Capital City Jazz Band. circa 1949. l-r: Jack Crook, Hal Swan, Jim Herrilson, Joe Miller, Otto Dicks and Tom King. A very popular group in the Sacramento area.

opposite

Burt Bales with Slim Evans and Slim's wife Billie on washboard. At this gig they entertained by playing any requests, but according to Burt they were not allowed to play jazz. This is one of the frustrations of being a jazz musician, but a job is a job.

above

Bob Scobey's Jazz Band at the Melody Club. l-r: Squire Girsback, Burt Bales, Jack Buck, Bill Dart, Bob Scobey and Jack Crook. Notice the white circle above Burt Bales. Scobey removed the sign that advertised Pat Patton's Frisco Jazz Band.

below

The Dude Martin country band (or western swing as it was then known) was very popular in the Bay Area and Dude often had jazz artists such as Squire Girsback, Burt Bales and shown here, Red Gillham, playing with his band. Ted Johnson was the band's manager as well as the accordion player. Later he owned a music store in San Leandro. The piano player, Al "Professor" Eisler, was one of Pete Clute's teachers.

above

One of Turk's earliest recordings by his band and the tune he played for Maria and Jim Goggin when they married. For the record, Turk, born Melvin Murphy, got his nickname while playing sports at Williams High School in Williams California. He was born in Palermo, California.

right

Hangover Club's sign, February 1950. The Hangover Club was a very popular jazz club located on Bush and Powell Streets in San Francisco. Many well-known musicians worked there. We believe Larry Quilligan was the photographer.

inset

Hangover Club Cocktail Napkin.

far right

On the bandstand at Hangover Club, February 1950 l-r: Stan Ward, Wingy Manone, Tom Marks and Turk Murphy.

CHAPTER 3

THE 50s TWO-BEAT GOES ON

In the summer of 1951, Turk's band followed Bob Scobey's band into the Greenwich Village in Palo Alto, California. The Village was a pleasant supper club with a unique parking arrangement. It adjoined a used car lot also run by owners Barney Apfel, his wife and Sid Weiss. At night, when the lot closed, Barney and Sid would move the cars to the back of the lot, cover the used car billboards with free parking signs, and invite the shopping public. Since parking in Palo Alto in that shopping district was as difficult as it is in present day San Francisco, the Greenwich Village always looked like standing room only, until the club's doors opened. For all it's plusses, it just couldn't survive a five-night week. With Chapter 11 staring at them, the owners did something bizarre in the history of club closings. They tossed a free champagne buffet supper, shut the doors and partied with the band and guests until the food and drink was consumed.

above

Photo in front of the Hangover Club with "Doc" Dougherty, the owner, and Maria Cuthbertson, the hatcheck girl, now Maria Haas.

right

Photo taken in an Francisco April 25, 1950. On the left is Nesuhi Ertegun who with his brother Ahmet, recorded the Yerba Buena Jazz Band, Bunk Johnson, Jelly Roll Morton, Kid Ory and others on the Jazz Man label. On the right is Larry Quilligan a jazz fan who writes for jazz periodicals. Larry also supplies jazz recordings to the Florida school system.

The Clayton Club in downtown Sacramento was the next stop on a planned agency tour for Turk's band, including Denver and the Blue Note in Chicago. The Sacramento date was memorable as an enjoyable gig with old friends sitting in, but especially because of a new singer who stunned the band.

Word had gotten around about Claire Austin, but no one expected a guest to sit in and do a couple of vocals associated with Bessie Smith and Ma Rainey. The engagement was a short one, as the next stop in Denver was a long car jump, but the stint at the Zanzibar in Aurora, Colorado turned out to be where and when the Fat Lady sang for the hopeful Murphy group.

That necessary nemesis of musicians, the booking agency, did its "strand act," Bob Helm recalls. "After sitting around watching the grits jar going empty along with the gas gauge needle, the "Don't call us, we'll call you" rang empty, so there was nothing left to do but split for homebase." Some members headed for Portland, Oregon, others to Los Angeles, and the rest returned to the Bay Area.

Charles Campbell, owner of the Campbell-Thiebaud Gallery, who had migrated to San Francisco in the 40s and by then had become one of the jazz scene's most enthusiastic collectors and supporters, persuaded Turk to put a band together for a San Francisco Hot Jazz Society date on January 6, 1952. Turk had called Campbell to come to Sacramento and hear Claire Austin and Campbell wanted a way to showcase her and Turk's band in San Francisco.

Campbell found the Italian Village on Columbus Avenue in San Francisco. The Village's main room supper club featured headliners, a floor show, chorus line and full-time orchestra for dancing. The basement and bar club was not being used. Campbell persuaded the owner to rent him the basement for a split on drinks.

The concert "was a smash," exclaims Campbell. The group that night consisted of Monte Ballou, Don Kinch, Bob Short and Bob Helm who were working in Portland at Monte's Diamond Horseshoe. While Kinch was at the Club Portland, Claire Austin came down from Sacramento and Wally Rose completed the pick-up group.

The turn out and enthusiasm generated by the Club's concert had impressed the Italian Village management and Campbell. They soon had a deal to make this a regular thing and what turned out to be a long run. "People lined up for blocks to get in," remembers Campbell.

It was a lot of fun, but a struggle to break even, says Campbell. "We had to watch every cent. We charged 75 cents at the door, something unusual in those days for a jazz club," he recalls. "Some people tried to avoid paying by claiming to be friends of Turk. I'd tell them in that case they'd have to pay double." Campbell adds. There was also a stiff 20% entertainment tax.

Meanwhile in Portland, jazz suffered a setback when the city served the Diamond Horseshoe management with a noise abatement complaint from the theater adjoining allowing Monte Ballou only a piano player, which put an end to the quartet and the weekend full band. Portland's loss was San Francisco's gain. As a result, Campbell was able to engage Turk and four pieces to start in the Spring of 1952.

Charles Campbell was joined by Bill Mulhern and assisted by wives, girlfriends and enthusiastic contributors in opening the Italian Village basement with Turk, Rose, Short, Lammi, and Helm. The Club supplied enough to sustain the five-piece group and give it time for repertoire growth along with featuring Claire Austin on weekends. The nucleus of former Yerba Buena Jazz Band members was able to revive former numbers and quickly implement old and new compositions and arrangements into cohesive and consistent performances.

Much original material and new arrangements were added at that time; obscure Morton, Oliver, Hot Five and Seven, Bessie Smith and Ma Rainey numbers plus rare rags. The Charles Campbell tape collection contains many examples of the small band's performances on unused tracks. Some of these were used as reference guidelines for future recording sessions by larger later groups.

Other clubs opened. Peggy Tolk-Watkins, opened the Tin Angel and later the Fallen Angel (it had been owned by that celebrated lady of the evening and once-Sausalito mayor Sally Stanford). Scobey, Helm and others played there. Jazz wasn't always on the billboard, though. A young singer named Johnny Mathis got his start there, and Odetta perfomed too.

San Francisco was a city that loved diversity. There could be bebop, the complex gyrations of modern jazz, rhythm 'n' blues, beatniks reading poetry at the Coexistence Bagel Shop, opera belted out in North Beach cabarets—and still there was room for traditional jazz to carve out its niche and begin to flourish.

The 1952-53 years of comparative obscurity in the subterranean sanctum came to an end in 1954 when Child's Paramount in New York City offered a date and Columbia Records another session. Trad jazz came, at least figuratively, above ground. It was discovered, and crossed over, at least momentarily, into the mainstream. The Village basement was filled by a talented group headed by Jim Leigh called the Eldorado Jazz Band and included Carol Leigh, Dan Rudger, Jim Borkenhagen, Squire Girsback, Russ Gilman, and Roland Working.

The Southland Swings

By 1950, the Southland's climate, easy lifestyle and performance opportunities attracted Eastern jazz musicians, so we really had the best in our backyard. The encroaching new sounds of cerebral bebop, progressive jazz, and the attendant coffeehouses competed with but didn't drown out traditional jazz. Real jazz thrived at the Hangover Club, Mike Lyman's, Sardi's, Brass Rail, Billy Berg's, Royal Room, 400 Club and the long-enduring Beverly Cavern.

On almost any night in 1950, one had the delightful dilemma of choosing between Kid Ory, Muggsy Spanier, Jack or Charlie Teagarden, Red Nichols, Ben Pollack (who had his own place on the Sunset Strip), Pete Daily, Nappy Lamare, even the Firehouse Five Plus Two upon occasion. It was not unusual to be able to sample touring groups at some of those clubs like George Lewis from New Orleans, Eddie Condon, even Louis Armstrong's All Stars. Besides headliners like these, the woods were alive with second liners, many of who were destined to come into their own in later years.

Several jazz clubs, many still active, were born in the Southland during the 50s—such was the popular appeal of jazz. And the first of what we now recognize as organized jazz festivals came with the Bull Norman Jubilee at the Pan-Pacific Auditorium in 1948. In 1960, it was Walt Disney's own idea to commit his whole park to a "Dixieland at Disneyland", which was good for a nine-year run.

However, by the end of the 50s there was a noticeable, disturbing decline in interest. A concatenation of circumstances found rock n' roll siphoning off the younger audiences and, one by one, jazz spots as we knew them, began posting unfamiliar names on their tote-boards, or simply closed their doors and put out the lights due to lack of support.

—-K.O. Eckland

opposite

Dr. Hayakawa, later a U.S. Senator, was well known in the jazz world for his lectures. He often used Bob Scobey's band or Turk's band. Notice the spelling of Murphy's name on this circa 1950s poster.

below

Burt Bales, Billy Newman and Jack Minger at the Hangover Club in San Francisco. Billy, an exceptional musician, spent many years as a studio musician in Hollywood, but found some time to record with Turk Murphy, Bob Scobey and others. Jack Minger is still an active musician.

above

Jack Sheedy Jazz Band. l-r: Bert Pearl, Bill Dart, Jack Minger, Paul Miller, Pat Patton and Jack Sheedy. Bill Erickson played piano in this band. Photograph from the collection of Ed Lawless who was given these photos by Patsy Patton. She did not know who took the picture. The Sheedy Band recorded about twenty sides on 78s including an interesting version of *Lady Maud's Dream*.

left

The Hangover Club house band performing at San Quentin in 1951 under the sponsorship of the American Federation of Variety Artists. l-r: Dave Lario, Skipp Morr, Marty Marsala, Smokey Stover, Albert Nicholas and Joe Sullivan. Burt Bales considered the Scobey recordings with Nicholas the best sides by Scobey. His favorite was *Beale Street Mama*. Photo courtesy of Maria Haas.

right

Post cards announcing jazz performances. In the 50's a post card could be mailed for one cent so they were a major means of keeping jazz fans informed. These were Bayside Jazz Society productions. This society was formed to satisfy those who did not want to go to San Francisco, by Ray Boarman, Dick Krause, Ken McLaughlin and Jim Goggin. Jenny Lind Hall in Oakland had a great sound.

below

Ad for Burt Bales at Victor's and Roxies. January 20, 1951. One of the band members was Pat "Hots" O'Casey who also worked with Jack Fina and Bob Scobey. You never knew what "Hots" might do. It was not unusual for him to take a solo in a horizontal position.

above

Photo of The Social Polecats, ca 1950s. l-r: Bob Hoskins (you can almost see him) Howard Wood, Bunky Colman, Bunnie O'Brien, Dick Oxtot, K.O. Eckland, Bob Bissonette. The Polecats, founded by Eckland, recorded some 78s for their own label and worked in various clubs including Victor and Roxie's in Oakland. K.O. was also with the Firehouse Five Plus Two and is currently with Hal Smith's Frisco Syncopators.

below

Photo of Pat "Hots" O'Casey on clarinet shown with l-r: Paul Lingle, Jack Minger, Turk Murphy, Bill Newman and Squire Girsback.

right

This September 1980 photo by Jim Goggin could have been taken in 1951 as the club had not changed. Roxie's name never was on the sign. Scobey worked in this club for quite some time.

right

This grouping of postcards indicates some of the jazz activity in the early 50s.

The Great Jazz Revival

JAZZ EXTRAORDINARY!! *featuring*
TURK MURPHY'S JAZZ BAND

TURK MURPHY, Trombone WALLY ROSE, Piano MONTE BALLOU, Banjo
BOB HELM, Clarinet DON KINCH, Trumpet BOB SHORT, Bass

and introducing for the first time in San Francisco . . .
CLAIRE AUSTIN
Singing in the tradition of Bessie Smith and Ma Rainey

SUNDAY AFTERNOON - JANUARY 6th 1952 - 2 to 6
ITALIAN VILLAGE — 915 COLUMBUS AVE. AND LOMBARD STREET

Admission $1.20 - DANCING - COCKTAILS

right

Claire Austin photo circa 1950s. Very popular singer who recorded with Turk Murphy and Kid Ory. She also had her own LP with Bob Scobey as sideman.

left

Claire Austin at the Italian Village. l-r: Turk Murphy, Claire Austin, Willie Thorpe, Monte Ballou, Wally Rose, Bob Short, Don Kinch, and Bob Helm. She was a smash!

left

Photo taken at the Italian Village in the 50s. l-r: Ann Fitzgerald (later Jack Crook's wife), Esther Campbell, Sanford Neubauer, Charles "Duff" Campbell (Turk Murphy composed *Duff Campbell's Revenge* for an Eddie Condon recording. It was a difficult key to play in and they struggled with it. Since Charles did not like Condon's style of playing Turk Murphy thought the title was appropriate!), Janet Richards and Charlie Richards. Photo courtesy of Charlie Richards.

right

Poster for the Italian Village.

left

Photo of Edmond Hall and Ralph Sutton taken at the Hangover Club in the 1950s probably by Marilyn Napier McGwynn.

right

Gene Norman's Southern California presentation of *Just Jazz* in the 1950s, a very well-run series of concerts. l-r: circa 1954 – George Probert (this superb soprano saxophonist is still featured at jazz festivals), Jack Buck, Marty Napoleon, Bob Scobey, Trummy Young, Louis Armstrong, and the hand of Freddie Higuera. The photographer was possibly Larry Kostka. This photo was a gift from Clancy Hayes.

left

Columbia recording session, August, 1953. Shown are Turk Murphy, Bob Short and Bob Helm. This is the session where Fred Crewes was listed as playing tuba, which never happened. Crewes, a blind piano player who worked in various clubs, was a friend of the band and received a recording fee as he needed funds at the time. Bob Short played trumpet and later dubbed in the tuba parts.

left

Cover of Sixth Annual Dixieland Jubilee program, October 1953. Autographed by Sidney Bechet.

below

Sidney Bechet with the Bob Scobey Band, October 1953 at the Frank Bull and Gene Norman Dixieland Jubilee in Los Angeles. l-r: Jack Buck, Bob Hotaling (possibly), Sidney Bechet, (bass player unknown), Bob Scobey, Clancy Hayes and Burt Bales. This photograph was a gift from Clancy Hayes who thought the photographer was Ray Avery, a well-known record store owner in Glendale, California.

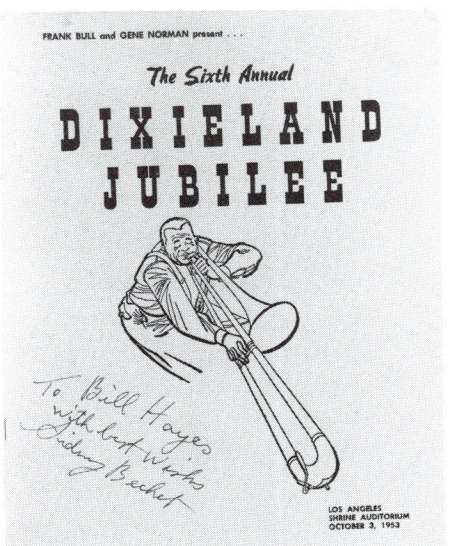

right

This is one of the best photographs ever taken of Bob Scobey. Harry Bowden took this on July 25, 1953 on the ferryboat Fort Sutter. From the collection of Charles Campbell. Bob's middle name was Alexander which was also the name of his son. His first recording after the YBJB was for the Trilon label and the band's name was Alexander's Jazz Band with the leader's name, R. Alexander Scobey. Bob also used the name Alexander for the brief period he owned the former Hambone Kelly's.

'The Old Man on Eddy-st' Is Dead

His Record Shop Was World Famous

"The Old Man on Eddy-st," known to record collectors around the world, is dead.

Few of them ever knew his name, William Melander, but they turned to his cluttered little shop for scarce records, anything from Haydn quartets to Turk Murphy.

He Knew His Stock

For 33 years he had built up his stock of records at 172 Eddy-st, piling them higher and higher toward the ceiling until there were only dark, dusty tunnels—but he knew where to put his hand on any record a customer wanted.

His own musical interests ranged from the classics to hot jazz, and many musicians came to his obscure shop to look for their own early recordings—Louis Armstrong, Bing Crosby, Ted Lewis.

Two Sisters Survive

Mr. Melander is survived by two sisters, Mrs. Florence Bacigalupi, at whose home he lived, at 34 Joice-st, and Mrs. Ida Holmstedt of Portland, Ore.

He was a member of Presidio Parlor 194, Native Sons of the Golden West.

Services will be held at 2 p.m. tomorrow at Halsted & Co., 1123 Sutter-st. Burial will be in Cypress Lawn Memorial Park.

left

Article about "The Old Man on Eddy Street" which appeared in the September 18, 1953 issue of The San Francisco News. What the article did not include was that Bill Melander, the "Old Man" was a former Shakesperian actor before he retired and went into the record business.

above

Photo of Bill Melander with an unidentified person in front of his store on Eddy Street. Norman Pierce purchased the inventory for his store Jack's Records. Pierce also did much for jazz by recording Burt Bales and providing a meeting place for jazz record collectors.

right

Newspaper article about *Clancy's Corner*, a weekly television show on KPIX, San Francisco.

below

Clancy's Corner, 1954. l-r: Clancy Hayes, Burt Bales, Bob Scobey, Jack Buck, Dick Lammi and Bill Napier. Photographer was probably Marilyn Napier McGwynn.

PAGE 18   Tuesday, June 22, 1954   CCCCAA
THE SAN FRANCISCO CHRONICLE

Television And Radio
By TERRENCE O'FLAHERTY

'Clancy's Corner' Is A Happy, Short Show

THE swinging doors flew open with a bang last week to start the new KPIX show "Clancy's Corner," with Clancy Hayes, Bob Scobey and the Frisco Jazz Band. It turned out to be a happy ten-minute show of continuous music provided by six musicians who know what they're doing.

If you like jazz of the "Everything Is Peaches Down in Georgia" variety, you'll like this. Probably the neighbors won't, because it comes on at 10:50 tonight and every Tuesday on KPIX. The show could stand a little more imagination shown in production and direction; otherwise, it's noisy, good-natured — and offers the viewer an easy way to go to bed in a happy mood.

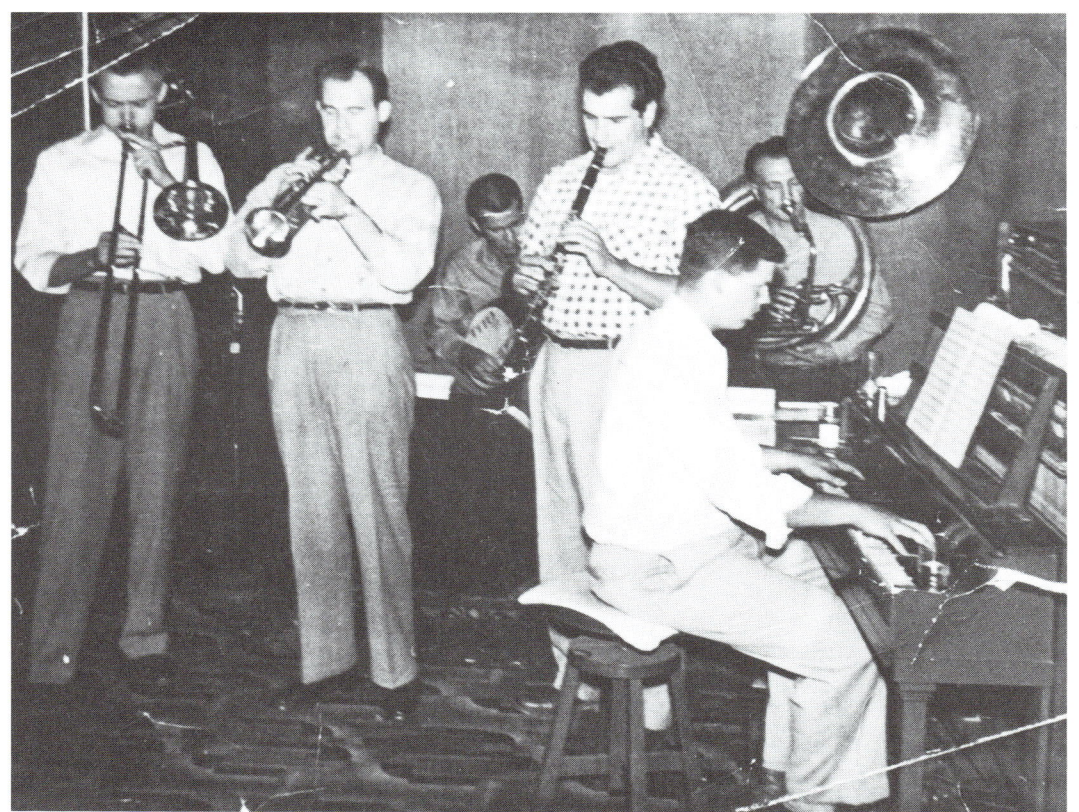

left

The Canal Street Jazz Band circa 1954. l-r: Sanford Neubauer, Al Cavallin, Tito Patri, Roy Giomi, Pete Clute and Don Longbella. They performed at the Italian Village when Turk was on an eastern tour, the Sail 'N as well as other San Francisco clubs. Pete joined Turk's band in January 1955.

clockwise from top

The Tin Angel, trombonist Charlie Richards in front. Tin Angel tent card. Half-price pass for Turk Murphy. Newspaper ad for Bob Scobey appearing at the Tin Angel in San Francisco circa 1954. Photo of Tin Angel courtesy of Charlie Richards.

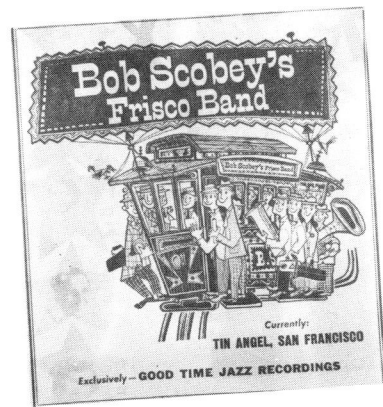
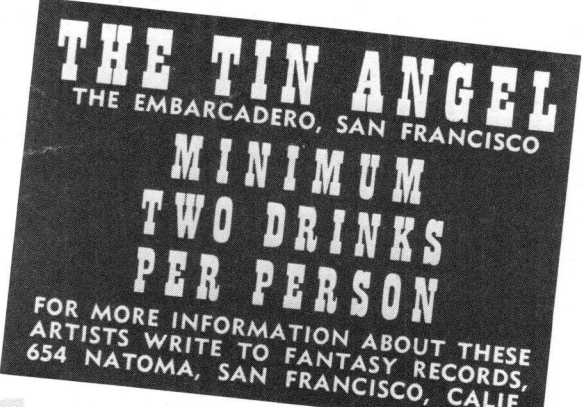

above

Photo of Lotte Lenya of *Mack the Knife* fame with Turk Murphy circa 1950s. She recorded *Mack the Knife* with Turk Murphy for distribution in Germany and it became a big seller there. Turk Murphy, as requested by Columbia A&R man George Avakian, did an arrangement for Louis Armstrong of the same song. Neither Louis or Turk thought the song would go anywhere so Turk took a flat fee of $300.00. Louis left shortly after the recording session for Europe and was amazed, upon his return, that the tune was a smash with over one million copies sold. They did not have a copy of the score so they went to a place with a juke box to re-learn the tune.

below

Record label for *Mack the Knife*.

below

Photo of Turk Murphy Band circa 1954. l-r: Turk Murphy, Ev Farey, Al Lyons, Bob Short, Bob Helm and Wally Rose. Ev roomed with Al while on the road, but had little sleep as Al's dog would chew on bones all night. Fortunately for Ev, Al Lyons was not with the band very long.

right

Flyer for the Hunt Club, Berwyn, Illinois, November 1955. Turk did not like "Frisco" being used for San Francisco, but a job is a job! Bill Carter, the clarinetist, later played for the Magnolia Jazz Band.

left

Reverend Alvin Kershaw of Oxford, Ohio a contestant in the *$64,000 Question* television quiz show, October 1955. l-r: Turk Murphy, Pete Clute, "Doc" Evans, Dick Lammi, Bill Carter and Thad Vandon (hands barely visible). If you are really into trivia you will want to know that the Reverend elected to bow out after winning $32,000 rather than chancing a miss at $64,000.

right

Photo of LP cover of Bob Helm's Riverside Roustabouts. The album consisted of eight sides of original tunes by Weldon Kees and Bob Helm. The group was able to play hot yet have a light touch. Well worth having in a jazz collection. There has been renewed interest in England concerning the poetry of Weldon Keees. Unfortunately, he died before this happened.

The Great Jazz Revival

right

Drawing for Ralph Gleason article about Marty Marsala, November 23, 1958. The band consisted of Marty on trumpet, Skipp Morr trombone, Vince Cattolica clarinet, Cuz Cousineau drums, Ernie Figueroa bass, and Tiny Crump piano. They were well received at the Kewpie Doll on Broadway, San Francisco.

left

Photos of Lu and Pat Watters taken in Cotati by Walter Knight in 1959. By that time Lu had been out of the music business for sometime. Pat Watters played an active role at Hambone Kelly's.

top

Bob Mielke and his Bearcats. Photo taken by Ed Salzman at Reno's in Oakland, 1956. l-r: Dick Oxtot, Pete Allen, P.T. Stanton, Bunky Colman and Bob Mielke. The Bearcats recorded for Empirical Recordings of Ohio in 1954 at the Jenny Lind Hall in Oakland. The recording supervisor sent Bob Mielke a few dubs of the recording and then disappeared with the masters. To this day, Bob has no idea what happened. In any event the sides were finally made available by using the dubs and the musicians (or heirs) were paid. The recording, issued by the San Francisco Traditional Jazz Foundation on its own label, was made possible by a grant from Maria Goggin and Bill Tooley.

bottom

This photo of Kid Ory with his daughter is one of our favorites. It was taken in 1956 at Ory's residence in San Anselmo, California by Robert A. Brunner and was donated to the San Francisco Traditional Jazz Foundation by Walter Knight.

left

Photo taken in the 1950s of bassist Ed "Montudi" Garland, cornetist Pete Daily, guitarist/banjo player Johnny St. Cyr and pianist Alton Purnell.

below

Ad for Pete Daily, March 7, 1958. Pete also worked in the Hangover Club.

below

Exterior view of Easy Street, 1958.

right

Postcard about Easy Street, January 9, 1958. The idea behind Easy Street was to provide a home base for Turk's band. When they were on the road other jazz bands, including Louis Armstrong's, came in for two or more weeks.

left

Photo of Louis Armstrong and Turk Murphy, 1958. This appeared in a San Francisco newspaper. The caption read "Sports car fans will find it difficult to concentrate on the personalities in this photo, but brief study will reveal the presence of Louis Armstrong and Turk Murphy. The latter greeted Armstrong when the trumpeter arrived in San Francisco for a string of appearances. The auto, a Mercedes-Benz 300 SL, was Armstrong's means of transportation during his west coast sojourn."

right

Calling card for Bob Short. Herb Caen wrote in his column: "Mrs. R.L. Jr., member of one of S.F.'s most distinguished families, got so carried away while listening to Turk Murphy's Jazz Band in the Italian Village basement, that she whipped out one falsie and flung it into Bob Short's tuba; and then went right on dancing, bravely but lopsidedly."

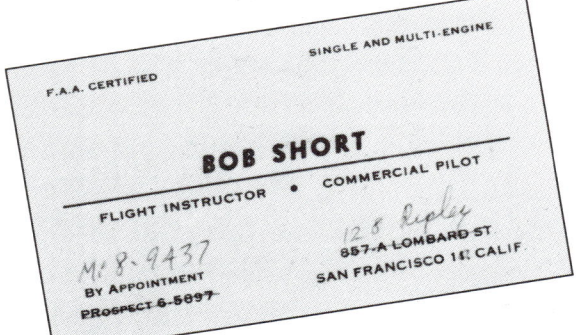

below left

Bob Short and Pat Patton, 1961.

below right

Bob Short, circa 1950's. Bob was an avid flyer—he even taught Bunky Colman how to fly. But sadly, he was killed in a plane crash. Photo donated by E. "Shorty" Short.

left

What do some musicians do when they leave jazz? Russ Bennett, the banjo player on YBJB sides fronted the house band at the Lake Merritt Hotel in Oakland for years. And here is Russ (on the left) handcuffed to Burt Lancaster. Russ was an extra for the movie *Birdman of Alcatraz*. "Easiest gig I ever had," Russ said. The movie was released in 1962.

right

The first Earthquake McGoon's located at 99 Broadway, San Francisco formerly the Sail 'N, opened September 27, 1960. If you knew the hand pointing out the club name was done by the banjo player Carl Lunsford, you get an A plus!

CHAPTER 4

THE 60S DIFFERENT DRUMMERS: TRAD JAZZ SPREADS

Turk Murphy and Pete Clute were walking around Times Square in New York one muggy summer night in 1960. They'd been on the road for 18 months. In fact, they'd been on the road together, off and on, since 1955. That was the year Wally Rose, Turk's pianist, decided he'd had enough of the road himself, so when Turk asked him to go to New York, he said no. As his replacement, Rose proposed one of his young, talented students—Clute—a kid Turk had often seen hanging out in the basement at the Italian Village in San Francisco, listening, listening. It had been a great series of road trips after that. In St. Louis and elsewhere they shared a stage with Dizzy Gillespie, Oscar Peterson and other jazz greats of the time.

But now the charm had worn thin for Murphy and Clute. They were homesick for the cool summer fogs of San Francisco. "We decided to open our own place, because that was the only way to guarantee we could stay in San Francisco and play the kind of music we wanted to play," recalls Clute. They'd saved up a little money and pressed a few friends for a bit more—just enough for a shoestring start.

They needed a name. "Earthquake" kept coming up. It was San Francisco and it was rollicking. They mulled over some of the options: Earthquake Bill's… Earthquake Bob's… *The* Earthquake… Earthquake Malone's—*Earthquake McGoon's!* They realized later that one reason Earthquake McGoon's sounded so right was that it had been the name of a character in Al Capp's *Lil' Abner* comic strip. Later they found out it also had been the nickname of a legendary World War II bomber pilot from Oakland—and that was perhaps where Capp got the name in the first place. They wrote Capp for permission. "As long as you play good music and keep your nose clean, you're welcome to the name," Capp wrote back.

Back in San Francisco they rented an old waterfront saloon at 99 Broadway, adjacent to the Embarcadero at the foot of Telegraph Hill. They opened the doors in September, 1960. Two young candidates, Jack Kennedy and Richard Nixon were squared off in the final months of a close presidential campaign. People still dressed up to go downtown in San Francisco; women wore white gloves. Beat poets roosted in North Beach. Rock'n'Roll was dawning. Four years and a presidential assassination later, the Beatles would land in America and a decade of protest, love-ins, acid, Woodstock, revolution, political, social and racial struggle would wash over San Francisco and the rest of the country.

"It was always difficult to make money playing the kind of music we played, but it was particularly difficult in the 60s," Pete remembers. "In the mid-fifties all kinds of new sounds were attracting the younger audiences. There was "cool jazz" and "be-bop" and then the Las Vegas style top forty out of which rock-'n'roll gradually evolved. We were already bucking all of those trends. Then came the Beatles."

In Los Angeles, things were a little better for trad jazz musicians. According to K. O. Eckland, places like Zucca's, Honeybucket, Club 47, Jolly Coachman, Gaslight, Storyville, Astor's, Zebra Room, White Way Inn and Chariot Room all offered trad jazz. They headlined big names like Nichols, Daily and Teddy Buckner, sometimes new groups like Jelly Roll, El Dorado, Red Pepper and Tailgate Ramblers, or combos fronted by Nappy Lamare, Joe Darensbourg, Rosy McHargue, Bill Dods, Johnny Lucas, et al. Sunday sessions at typical places like Larchmont Hall or various Elks and Moose lodges offered afficionados anything from a remarkable to an incredible afternoon of jazz.

On the whole, and in San Francisco, however, trad jazz was in retreat. It took six months for Turk and Clute to break even at their new place as 1960 rolled into 1961. They never made a lot of money, but they perservered. Eventually the fans began to come in greater and greater numbers and Earthquake McGoon's continued to be the one and only notable place in town for trad jazz.

In 1962, the club had to make the first of several moves. Redevelopers had plans for the prime waterfront area that didn't include honky tonk. They were given 60 days to find a new spot. After scrambling around for a few weeks they lit on the William Tell Hotel at 630 Clay Street. It was a three-level dance hall, built in 1911, with a balcony on the second story overlooking a spacious dancefloor. The old store fronts surrounding the club created alcoves where people could listen to the music coming from inside. It was the perfect space and atmosphere for Turk and his band to call home.

In fact, moving turned out to be one of the best things that ever happened to them. The new location quickly became a jazz Mecca, crowded not only with locals, but a must-stop on the tour bus routes throughout the 60s and into the 70s as well. It was close to North Beach and Chinatown, and near the now long-gone, but colorful downtown produce mart. They were also near the City's financial district, which was thriving with restaurants and night spots. And there were other plusses. At Broadway there had been no dancing, no food and no kids. All that changed at 630 Clay. Families could come and enjoy dinners, served between 6 and 7 in the evenings. And because Earthquake McGoon's was now a restaurant and not a bar, the younger crowd could stay late, dancing until two.

Celebrities began to come. Assured of the band's discretion, they could float into the shadows and enjoy the music as well as their privacy. Other "regulars" might come by at least once a year, infrequent, perhaps, but steady, customers.

Although the place was always packed on the weekends, on the weekdays there were slimmer pickings. The band played every day and the musicians were never paid less than the union minimum, so all kinds of stratagems were devised to draw the public from Monday through Thursday. Eventually they set up a magic cabaret in the basement called the Magic Cellar, showcasing magicians, tarot readings and other (in the words of Pete Clute) "funky odd-ball stuff."

Among their many gigs, the band used to play at dedication ceremonies for new buildings that were going up all over town during the construction boom. You might say they were "wanted men." At a sports bar called Shanty's where the Transamerica building now stands, Turk and Pete played one of their strangest requests. The owner, Shanty Malone, had decided to close down on New Year's Eve. He had a Steinway piano for sale for $50 which Turk and Pete agreed to buy the following day. They showed up early and were rolling the merchandise over to Earthquake McGoon's when a paddy wagon pulled up. The suspicious officer "busted" them on the spot, loaded the piano into the back of the van, and took them downtown—then around town— singing songs and playing piano.

above

Photo of Turk Murphy Band 1959. l-r: The banjo player was "Peanuts" Fitch who liked to wear cowboy boots. For a gig in Nevada, he purchased a cowboy hat and a gun which he used to shoot holes in his new hat. He did not last long with the band. Pat Yankee, vocals, Turk Murphy, trombone, Jack Carroll, trumpet, Bob Helm, clarinet, Pete Clute, piano, and Bob Short, tuba. Photo taken by Jack Farrell in Virginia City, Nevada.

Through all the changes, the band and the music stayed pretty much the same. Besides Turk on trombone and Clute on piano, regulars included Bob Helm on clarinet, Ernie Carson on cornet, Bob Short, tuba, and Carl Lunsford, banjo. Pat Yankee sang and later started her own club with part of Turk's band at Mike's Pool Hall on Broadway. Occasionally a drummer would sit in, but it was hard to find anyone who wanted to lay back and just keep the beat (which is what trad jazz drummers had to do at least as far as Turk Murphy was concerned).

Even though the sixties were a tough time for trad jazz, at Earthquake McGoon's the band played on. They had a long run on Clay Street going strong right through 1979, when the band again had to move on because of redevelopment. A nondescript skyscraper squats at the location now. By then, however, the birth of festivals such as the Sacramento Jazz Festival in 1973 and renewed audience interest assured the continued preservation of the trad jazz sound.

left

On the Victor recording date Pete Clute played calliope on a few numbers. The volume of the calliope created all kinds of problems. Turk said: "We rented a calliope and brought it in the studio and recorded with that and proceeded to wreck RCA Studios and everything else. It was a day they would like to forget". (Turk's comments appeared in Jim Goggin's book *Turk Murphy-Just for the Record*).

below

Photo of Frankie Capp who played drums with The Turk Murphy Band on a Victor Recording, May 1 & 2, 1961. Frankie was considered to be a modern drummer, but he blended right in with the band. Frankie is still going strong — he played the 1994 St. Louis Mid-America Jazz Festival.

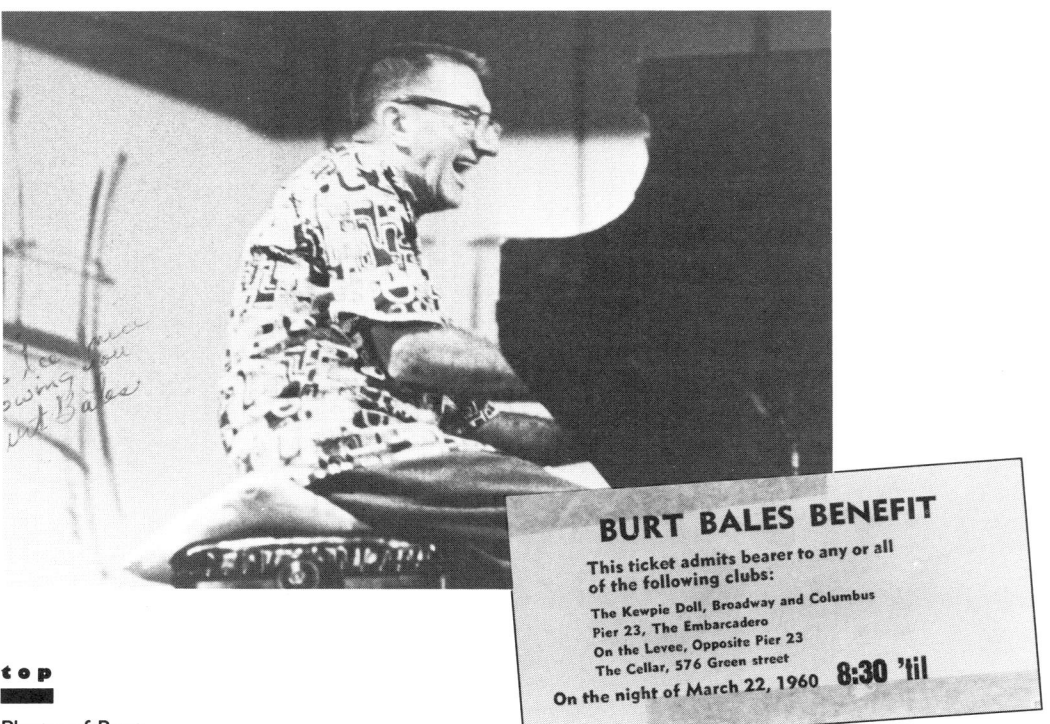

center

Burt Bales benefit ticket, March 22, 1960. Four jazz nightclubs and dozens of jazz musicians combined efforts in a benefit for Burt Bales who was hit by a car while jay walking. Included were Kid Ory, Marty Marsala's Chicagoans, Bob Mielke's Bearcats, Wally Rose and his band and more. This successful event was organized by Richard Hadlock. Over $2,000 was raised.

top

Photo of Burt.

bottom

Photo of Pier 23 on the San Francisco Embarcadero. The home base for Burt Bales over, in his words, "too many years." Every Sunday there was a jam session at "The Pier". Bill Napier, the excellent clarinet player, also worked there often. Pier 23 is still in operation.

The Great Jazz Revival

below

The Turk Murphy Jazz Band on stage in the hangar bay of the USS Coral Sea, October 17, 1961. The band enjoyed gigs like this. The Coral Sea adopted the band as their own.

right

Both sides of Turk Murphy's calling card. Ward Kimball, trombone player and leader of the Firehouse Five Plus Two created the calling card for Turk. Ward was a senior man in the Walt Disney organization.

"I just happened to bring my horn"

TURK MURPHY
(AND HIS SAN FRANCISCO JAZZ BAND)

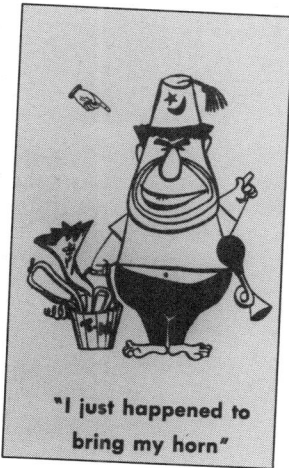

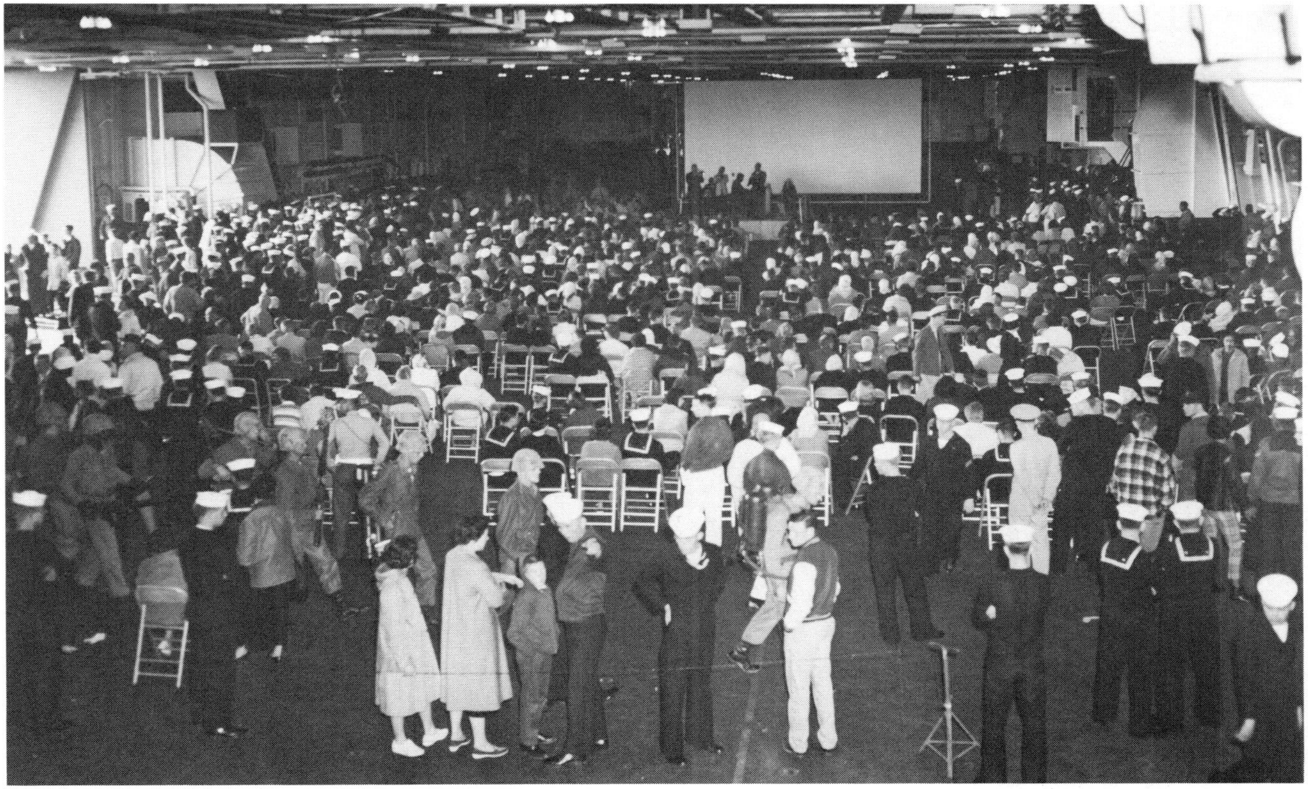

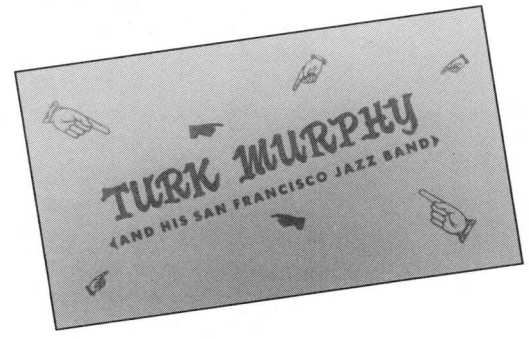

above

Pat Yankee and her Sinners band, circa 1962. She opened with this band at Mike's Pool Hall on Broadway in San Francisco. l-r: Ernie Carson, Bill Carroll, Art Nortier, Pat Yankee, Dave Wierbach, Bob Burkhart, Phil Howe. Pat played various clubs in San Francisco and Nevada. Pat also had a long run – from 1952-1956 – at Goman's Gay 90s, a very popular San Francisco club. Here's some trivia: Pat appeared in a 1946 movie called *It's Great to Be Young*.

above right

Cocktail napkin and matches from McGoon's.

left

Photograph of McGoon's with the Transamerica Pyramid in the background, circa 1960s. The early McGoon's ad contained the phrase, "McGoon's is so important they built a pyramid to mark its location."

above left

Flyer announcing the opening of the second Earthquake McGoon's on 630 Clay Street, San Franciscco, June 15, 1962. Not an easy opening as Turk had to replace musicians who were playing with Pat Yankee, but he did it and went on for years at this location which was Turk's favorite.

The Strange Story of Bob Scobey's Last Days

There's a strange story connected with the last days of Bob Scobey, who died of cancer recently.

Long before Scobey became ill, veteran New Orleans singer Lizzie Miles once vowed to the trumpeter that she would outlive him. By early this year, it appeared that the 67-year-old singer's prophecy was about to be fulfilled. Scobey, beyond medical help, was given but a few weeks to live, while Lizzie rested at home in comfortable retirement.

On March 17, the exact day of Lizzie Miles' sudden death, Scobey rallied and, to everyone's astonishment, went back to work at his Chicago club, Bourbon Street. Announcements of his "miraculous" recovery were sent out by the club.

It was, of course, a temporary victory. Yet, Scobey, found enough new strength to work through most of May, long after ordinary men would have given up. On his final day, June 12, the 46-year-old jazzman was making plans for his next job.

But this time he didn't make it. —R. H.

left

Article about the death of Bob Scobey, San Francisco Examiner, June 1963. The author was columnist Richard Hadlock who also played clarinet with Turk Murphy's Band in 1957–1958.

below

Publicity photo of Lizzie Miles, a gift of Clancy Hayes. Lizzie liked to include a Creole chorus in her songs. She dressed in gowns from the 1920s.

below

Photo of Paul Lingle as a boy. Paul Lingle was born into music as his father was a professional cornetist on the circuit. Paul played with Jimmie Grier's Band, although he preferred to be a soloist. As one of the early jazz pianists in San Francisco he became a legend. He was a staff musician for radio stations and was the pianist for Al Jolson in some of his movies. Paul was always reluctant to record so there are not too many recordings available.

below

Postcard announcing Lingle to perform at the Jug Club, circa 1950's. In the 50s Paul frequently performed at the Paper Doll.

above

Paul Lingle. He moved to Hawaii in the 1950s where he taught piano and played casuals. He died there in October 1962. "Pop" Kennedy, the president of Musicians' Union Local #6, helped arrange funds for his funeral expenses. By the way, Paul was a good friend of the famous Barbary Coast pianist Alameda Levy. Alameda passed on a lot of knowledge to the young Paul.

NOW BEING FEATURED AT
THE JUG CLUB
PAUL LINGLE
The Bay Area's
HOT DIXIE LAND JAZZ PIANIST
Thursday, Friday, Saturday and Sunday Nights
34th and SAN PABLO
PLENTY OF PARKING IN OUR LOT

below

Photo of the late Ralph J. Gleason and Jean Gleason by Sue Cassidy Clark. The Gleasons kept an open mind to all forms of music. He was a highly respected writer with the San Francisco Chronicle for many years.

right

Article about Lu Watters returning to the City by Ralph J. Gleason, San Francisco Chronicle, July 1963. Lu Watters played for a cause: the battle of conservationists against Pacific Gas & Electric Company's plans to build a nuclear power plant on Bodega Head.

Lu Watters Turns Back the Clock

Ralph J. Gleason

July 30, 1963

IT STARTED out as a benefit for the Association to Preserve Bodega Head and Harbor and the audience that jammed Earthquake McGoon's was motivated as much by the desire to overthrow the PG&E's plans as it was by nostalgia for the Dawn Club and Lu Watters.

But the evening wasn't half over before it evolved into a mass turn-back of the clock, a once-in-a lifetime excursion into Nostalgia City and a chance once more to relive those golden memories.

It couldn't have happened anywhere but in San Francisco. It took the homogeneity of the Bay Area, the proximity of Cal and Stanford and the fact that the graduates stay here, to breed a generation with the common memories and experiences of the Dawn Club-Hambone Kelly's class.

★ ★ ★

AND THEY were there at Earthquake McGoon's to see Lu Watters in the flesh again and to hear him play.

"I remember . . . I remember" was on everyone's lips. Grey-templed jazz fans kicked their heels on the floor, still articulating their objection to Glenn Miller as dance music. And it is part of the whole Lu Watter's culture that it is and was dance music.

A woman called early in the afternoon to know if she could bring her children and put them somewhere in sleeping bags. Peter J. Tamony went around showing tickets from 1940 of Dawn Club sessions with The Bay City Stompers and Lu and the Yerba Buena Jazz Band sponsored by the Hot Music Society of San Francisco. Vernon Alley, Ralph Sutton and Thad Vandam played a set and Barbara Dane sang with Al Zohn and Dick Hadlock backing her.

Hal MacIntyre introduced one set and for a moment the clock was really turned back 20 years to the old remote broadcasts from the Dawn Club.

The Great Jazz Revival

above

Photo by Walter Knight taken on July 28, 1963 for Bodega Bay benefit l-r: Bob Helm, Pete Clute, Lu Watters, Thad Vandon, Bob Neighbor, Bob Short, Turk Murphy and Dave Wierbach. Banjoist Ted Shafer of the Merry Makers label has released a recording of this concert. *See discography.*

right

Ticket for Bodega Bay Benefit, July 28, 1963. The day he closed the door at Hambone's, Lu gave away his horn but kept the mouthpiece, A fan, Don King, bought him a horn for this event. There was a second Bodega Bay Benefit in May 1964.

below

A still from the movie *Good Neighbor Sam* starring Jack Lemmon. The photograph was taken at Tommy's Joynt in San Francisco in October of 1963. Turk's Band can be heard for only a few seconds in the movie. The photographer was employed by Baylens of San Francisco. Band members shown are: Pete Clute (under Bob Helm's right elbow), Bob Helm, Thad Vandon (holding a banjo for effect only) Squire Girsback, Turk Murphy and Bob Neighbor.

above

A photograph of the Magic Cellar which was located in the basement of McGoon's. Shown are Pete Clute and Turk Murphy. The Magic Cellar housed a fabulous collection of memorabilia from Carter the Great, a popular magician who was also a partner of Harry Houdini. Carter performed throughout the early part of the century. The collection was discovered accidentally by Pete and Turk in an old garage they rented to store classic automobiles.

above

One of our favorite photographs of the Turk Murphy Band lined up in front of McGoon's bar. l-r: "Pancho" Lopez, Turk Murphy, Pete Clute, Squire Girsback, Thad Vandon, Bob Neighbor and Bob Helm. The nude above the bar was known as Mother McGoon but originally was used in an ad for Non Pareil Whiskey and titled *It's Up To You*. Photo by Russ Kelly, circa 1960.

top right

Label for a Motherlode 45 which was the in-house record label for McGoon's.

bottom right

Turk Murphy and Thad Vandon having fun while "Pancho" Lopez, long-time bartender at McGoon's watches. In the background is Cedric Clute (Pete's brother) who ran the Magic Cellar in the basement. Thad came from an entertainment family and Turk enjoyed his creativity and humor. Thad was also a good singer and one of Turk's favorite drummers. The two were responsible for the lyrics to a Goldwater For President recording on a 45 that was used for a theme of a San Francisco political rally.

below left

Photo of Firehouse Five Plus Two. L-r: Billy Newman, Frank Thomas, George Probert, Danny Alguire, Don Kinch, Eddie Forrest, Ward Kimball and George Bruns.

right

A flyer announcing the Firehouse Five Plus Two.

below right

Drawing by Ward Kimball.

right

This photo was a gift of Turk Murphy and shows the deep concern and love Louis Armstrong and Jack Teagarden had for clarinetist Pee-Wee Russell. Russell was greatly admired. He recovered from this hospital stay but passed away in 1969 at age 62. Pat and Patsy Patton cared for Pee-Wee at their home during one of his illnesses. The Pattons were quite generous.

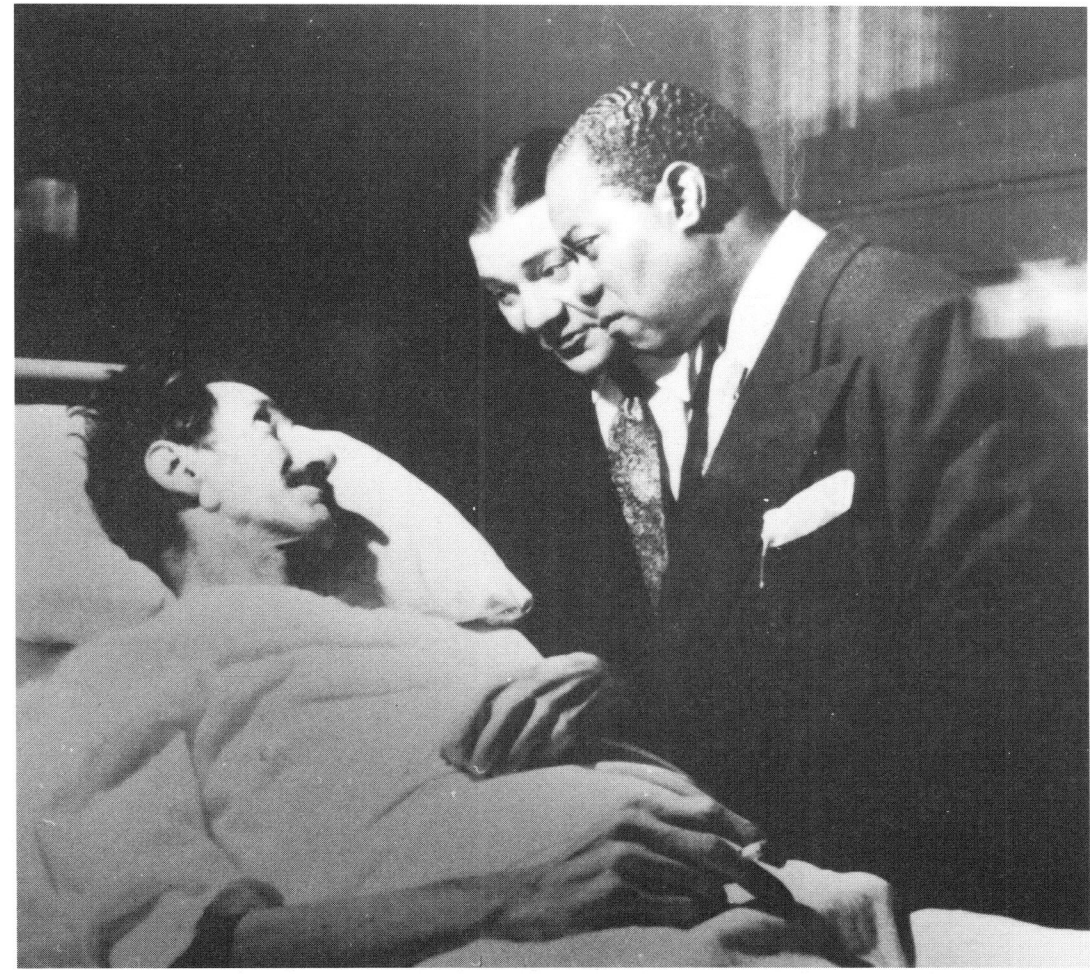

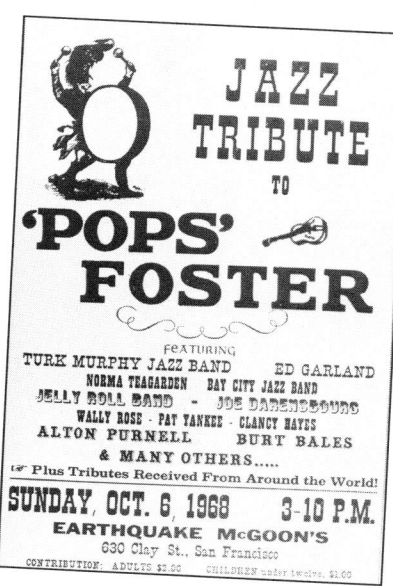

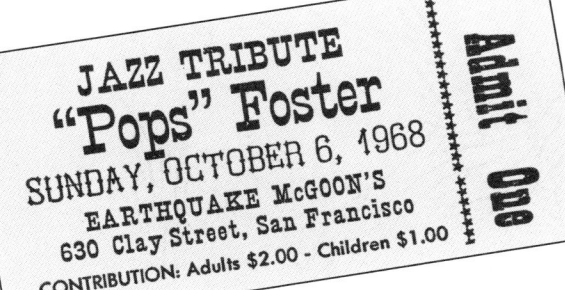

left

Ticket for "Pops" Foster tribute.

below

Photo of "Pops" Foster, date and photographer unknown, but we liked the photo.

above

Poster for Jazz Tribute to "Pops" Foster, October 6, 1968. This benefit brought responses from around the world. Ava Taylor (pianist Clarence William's widow) sent a generous contribution. "Pops" was pleased.

right

Memorial service for "Pops" Foster at Sacred Heart Church, San Francisco. His bass is displayed at the altar. Pops died on October 30, 1969. He was an historic jazz man who began playing the bass in Storyville. He played with all the greats, including Louis Armstrong, Kid Ory, Sidney Bechet, and Earl Hines and he probably made more jazz recordings than any other jazz musician. Turk Murphy's band played for the memorial service. Visible members are: Turk Murphy, Thad Vandon, Leon Oakley and Jack Crook.

above

The full Turk Murphy band behind Judith Durham, September 29, 1970 l-r: Phil Howe, Judith Durham, Leon Oakley, Jim Maihack, guest artist Woody Allen, Carl Lunsford, Turk Murphy and Pete Clute (barely visible). Judith, a gifted singer, composed a tune with Turk which regrettably was never recorded *Some Other Time*.

opposite

John Chancellor at McGoon's, January 1976. It was not unusual to see people like Allen, Chancellor, Walter Cronkite, or Bing Crosby at McGoon's.

CHAPTER 5

THE 70s 80s 90s
AND TOMORROW: TRAD JAZZ MARCHES TO THE MILLENIUM

The 1970s marked an ending and a beginning for trad jazz. The ending of an era was marked by the death of Louis Armstrong at 71 on July 7, 1971 in New York. *The Daily News* front page bannered: "SATCHMO DEAD, A JAZZ ERA ENDS." Other jazz greats were to go in the coming decades—Eubie Blake at 100 in 1983, and ultimately greats among the once-young San Francisco jazz revivalists themselves, including Lu Watters, Burt Bales and, on May 30, 1987, Turk Murphy at 71.

But trad jazz and the Great Jazz Revival did not die with them. Many of the original musicians, new musicians, new venues, new recordings, and new festivals carried the movement towards the 21st century. There was too much momentum to stop it now. Watters, Murphy, Scobey, et. al. had sounded the call and trad jazz had found a permanent niche in the pantheon of American popular culture.

By the start of the 70s, clubs showcasing trad jazz were down to a handful, but special occasion performances and jazz festivals started popping up. In San Francisco, Earthquake McGoon's remained an "in" place. Tour busses came every night and the patrons were often delighted to see celebrities in the audience. San Francisco Examiner & Chronicle columnist Bill Alex recalls the night the Count Basie Band came in. "Everyone thoroughly enjoyed themselves and the place was jumping."

In Southern California, Disneyland began featuring trad jazz as a staple. There were Shrine Auditorium concerts and one-day affairs at the Wilshire-Ebell Theater and Catalina Island became popular, ensuring continuity of the art.

The Sacramento Jazz Jubilee, established in 1973 would grow into a hugely successful annual bash. It would serve as a template for jazz club sponsored functions that began appearing in larger, more ambitious formats. The jazz revival played on everywhere, including some hallowed halls. Turk Murphy performed each Easter in San Francisco's magnificent Grace Cathredral. In January, 1987, just six months before his death, he played a packed Carnegie Hall to rave reviews, a long way from Earthquake McGoon's.

Just like the 70s, during the 80s, the number of jazz clubs continued to decrease while there was quite an increase in concerts and festivals. Unfortunately, for the professional musicians they were often asked to accept less than "scale" pay.

Even the venerable Earthquake McGoon's closed its doors in 1984 and the band moved up the hill to the Fairmont, but things were just not ever the same.

But the easy, lively beat of trad jazz goes on. Records, tapes and CDs continue to be released and re-released, festivals draw record-breaking crowds, performances brighten clubs, theme parks, joints and conventions. A lot of the playing these days can be a pallid imitation of the real thing as it used to be performed by the greats and the great revivalists. But some of it still is superb.

West coast traditional jazz societies are abundant, as are periodicals. Annie Street, where it all started at the Dawn Club at number 20, was rededicated in 1980 after years of anonymity as "Mark Twain Lane." In 1994, a small street in North Beach was named after Turk Murphy. Much music and celebration accompanied each ceremony.

Not that anyone needs street signs or road maps to find jazz anymore—the sounds emanate from all over. First there was jazz; then there was the Great Jazz Revival. Now copycats and lots of cats are around to keep on jiving and reviving it all. As we approach the millennium, *Trad Jazz, the Next Generation*, probably will be heard playing that great Murphy composition, *Minstrels of Annie Street*, and meaning every note of it, no longer on Annie Street, but somewhere out there, maybe even in outer space. That wouldn't be anything new either, though. They went into orbit a long time ago on Annie Street.

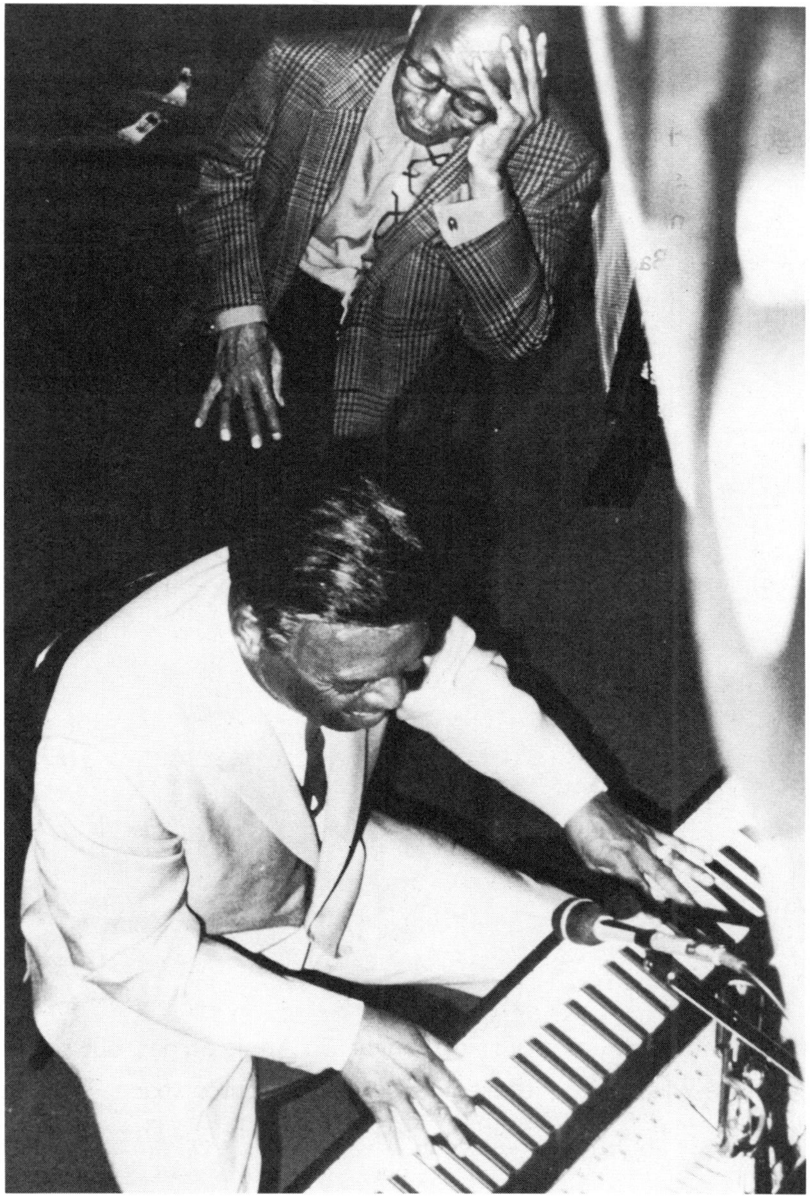

left

Photo of Earl "Fatha" Hines and Eubie Blake at McGoon's, March 28, 1971. Earl Hines is seen playing a tune, *Memories of You*, written by Eubie Blake. Needless to say, Eubie was impressed. The fabulous Fatha' played at the Hangover Club quite often in the 1950s. Hines did much to change the role of a piano in jazz. His big band was also popular.

below

Eubie Blake's logo.

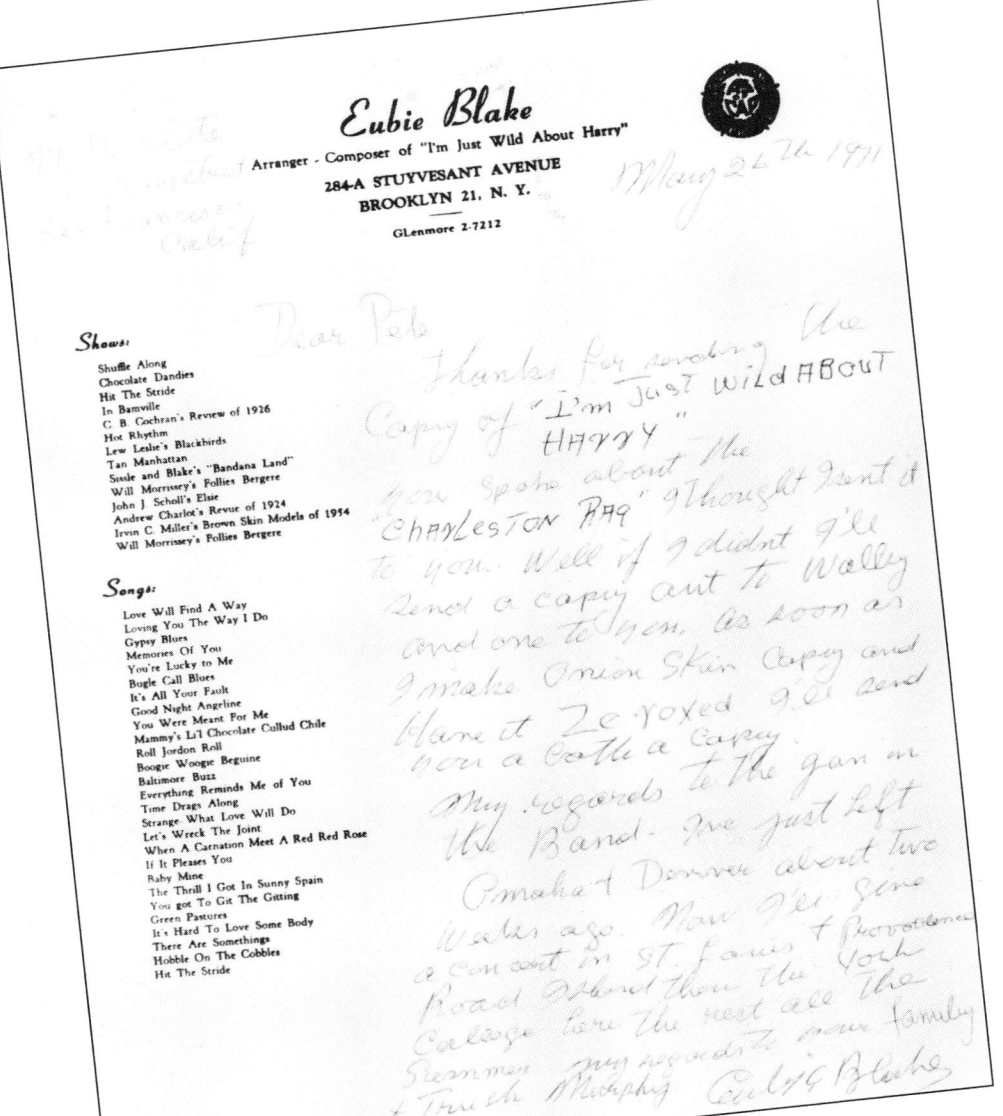

left

Letter from Eubie Blake to Pete Clute. What a delight it was to watch Eubie play the piano. His enthusiasm for music was infectious, and his many compositions are still being played.

'Queen Vee' Sings Again

By Philip Elwood

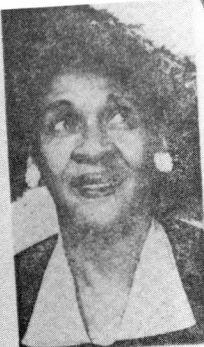

VICTORIA SPIVEY
Old time song stylist

Victoria Spivey, a gamey strong-voiced contalto who made something of a splash in the pop-blues world of the 1920s, has arrived at Earthquake McGoon's for a month's stay.

Miss Spivey, accompanied brilliantly by pianist Ray Skjelbred, is singing a cross section of the type of material that gained her some fame in olden times.

The "Queen Vee," as she used to be billed in vaudeville, is not a blues singer. Rather she always has been associated with stagey presentations, "blues type" tunes, double entendre lyrics and a straight forward and impersonal sort of delivery.

Her best material at McGoon's is the stuff from Bessie Smith's early repertoire. Numbers like "Gulf Coast Blues," "Careless Love," and "Baby Won't You Please Come Home."

Miss Spivey, for any age (and she admits to 65) looks great and dresses with taste and class. Her voice, firm and rich in the lower register, seems now to have a restricted range and wanders off pitch rather often.

She worked, way back, with all the greats — Louis Armstrong, Clarence Williams, King Oliver, Lonnie Johnson, and the rest.

But though associated briefly with jazz and blues personalities Miss Spivey was actually always more part of musical show-biz, vaudeville, and the talkies than of the jazz-blues world.

Her "T. B. Blues" (which she's still doing) and "No Papa No," "Funny Feathers," etc., were lively risque performances in the Depression era.

As a bandleader, singer, the theatrical personality Miss Spivey played most of the S.F. prior to World War II. Recently she has had a modest comeback, appearing on blues shows and making a number of nostalgic LPs.

At McGoon's she sings short intermissions, staging most of her numbers and portraying an entertainment world that is mostly forgotten today.

Skjelbred is a superb accompanist, rich in the James P. Johnson - Clarence Williams traditions, competent with Jelly Roll Morton arrangements and a notable asset to Miss Spivey.

below

Everyone mourned the passing of Louis Armstrong

above

Victoria Spivey appears at McGoon's. McGoon's also had a showing of *Hallelujah!*, an all black cast motion picture made by King Vidor and an early sound movie. It was way ahead of its time.

left

Spencer Quinn with air-pump horn, circa 1970s. Spencer was an intermission banjo player at McGoon's and was regarded as a good entertainer. He was an *Our Gang* kid in the 30s and spent his life in the entertainment world.

below left

David Fasken was one of the founders of the San Francisco Traditional Jazz Foundation. He was the producer of Turk Murphy's recording of *The Many Faces of Ragtime* and did much for jazz musicians.

below right

Bob Helm and Carl Lunsford circa 1970. If the canary (in the cage) died they took that as a bad omen.

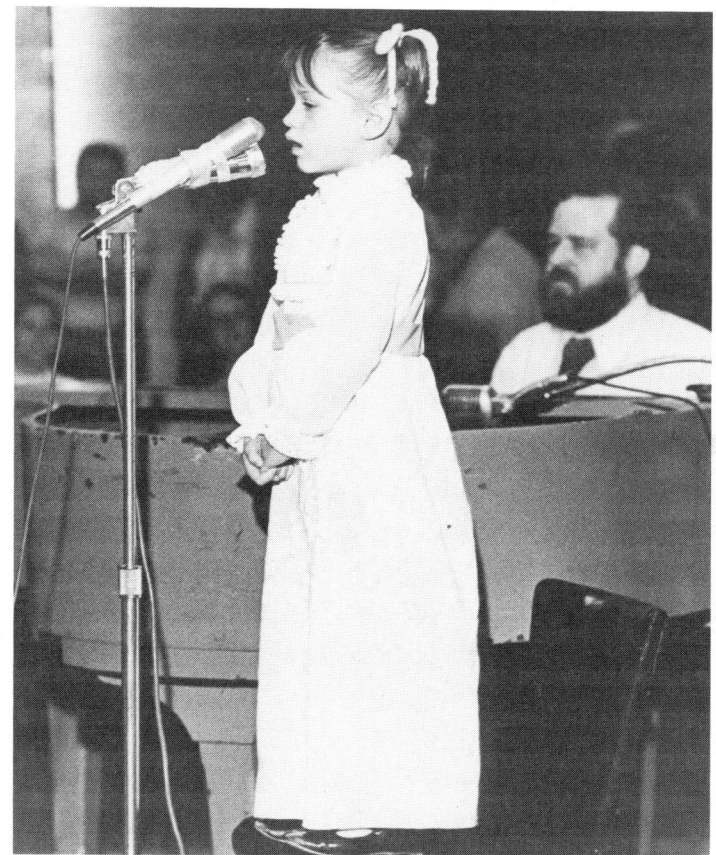

above

A very young Molly Ringwald with her dad, Bob Ringwald on piano. They recorded an LP together and Molly later went on to Hollywood. Bob is the leader of the Great Pacific Jazz Band. Circa 1970s.

right

The Oakland A's Muleskinners. Later they were called the Swingin' A's. Bob Mielke trombone, Bob Neighbor cornet, Bob Helm reeds, Dick Oxtot banjo and John Moore tuba.

below left

Clancy Hayes Day poster, June 13, 1971. Drawn by Sally Cruickshank.

below right

Letter from then Governor of California, Ronald Reagan.

right

Ticket for Clancy Hayes day. Clancy was ill with cancer and had an operation which left him needing money. The event helped him make ends meet.

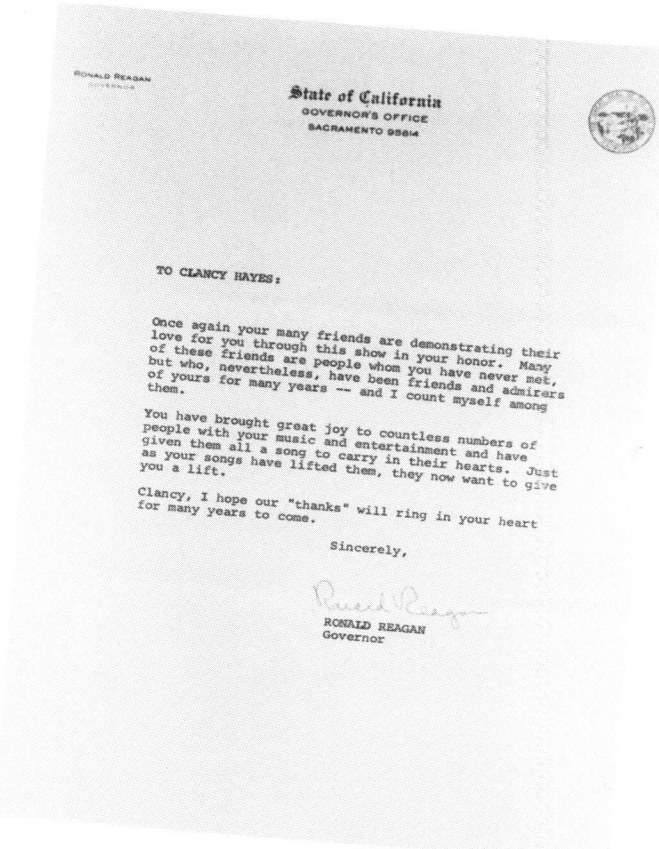

below

Clancy Hayes - with and without hair! Clancy joined NBC in 1929 and had many radio shows.

right

Wilbur Stump cartoon sent to Clancy while he was hospitalized. Wilbur was a well known pianist who played most clubs in the Bay Area.

left

This 1966 photograph was taken at McGoon's. l-r: Bob Neighbor, Turk Murphy, Jack Crook and Clancy Hayes. Clancy was the intermission artist at McGoon's. His set usually closed with the band members, one by one, joining in with him until the whole band was on stage, much to the delight of the audience. Here they are recording for Paramount Records. The album was *Clancy Hayes Live at Earthquake McGoon's*.

left

Photograph by Matt Southard of Clancy's memorial service, March 17, 1972. Headline from an article in the San Francisco Examiner.

Pat Patton

Pat Patton, banjo player and bassist — a popular performer in Bay Area jazz and dance bands for nearly 50 years — died on Monday, 2 days short of his 72nd birthday.

Patton was associated with the traditional jazz revival in the Bay Area in the 1940s and 1950s and organized the Frisco Jazz Band in 1945.

His colleagues in the Frisco Band included the late Clancy Hayes, vocalist; later on that band became trumpeter Bob Scobey's group.

Pat played and recorded frequently with various of the Lu Watters' Yerba Buena Jazz Bands and in recent years performed at most of the New Orleans Jazz Club's affairs.

A fine musician, respected gentleman and jazz authority.

— Philip Elwood

S.F. EX. 3/6/76.

left

Phil Elwood's article about the death of Pat Patton, San Francisco Examiner, March 6, 1976.

right

Obituary for Patsy Patton who died on February 3, 1993. While this is out of chronolgical order, we know Pat and Patsy would like it this way.

PATTON, Patsy — Died on Wednesday, February 3, 1993 at age 84; a native of San Francisco, born July 2, 1908; Patsy was a popular Caberet Singer and performer in the Bay Area jazz and dance bands; her late husband, Pat Patton was associated with the traditional jazz revival in the Bay Area in the 1940's and 1950's and organized the Original Frisco Jazz Band in 1945; his colleagues in the Frisco Band included the late Clancy Hayes; later on that band became trumpeter Bob Scobey's group; Lu Waters and Pat Patton formed a small rehearsal group in early 1940, which also included Turk Murphy, Bob Helm, Squire Girshback, and the late piano great Paul Lingle, which was the immediate forerunner of the famed Yerba Buena Jazz Band; may Patsy and Pat long enjoy jazz duets along with all the other late jazz greats; Patsy Patton is survived by her son, Robert; granddaughter Susan; family friend Dr. Edward Lawless & Patsy Waters, wife of the late Lu Waters.

No Services will be held. The family asks that donations in the memory of Patsy go to your favorite charity. Patsy and Pat say, 'Bye and see you later'

right

Photo of Pat Patton at Hambone Kelly's 1949. In this pick-up group are l-r: Pat "Hots" O'Casey, Bunky Colman, Pat Patton, Wingy Manone and Joe Zohn. Photo from the collection of Ed Lawless.

below

The Turk Murphy band moved to The Rathskellar in 1978. This was a temporary situation until the next McGoon's at 128 The Embarcadero in San Francisco was ready. Photograph by Ed Lawless. Ed and Dottie Lawless have spent a substantial portion of their lives preserving moments in jazz with their photography and they are known for their organizational abilities.

right

Photo of Turk Murphy Band with the Palace of Fine Arts as backdrop circa 1978. l-r: Pete Clute, Bill Carroll, John Gill, Bob Helm, Leon Oakley and Turk Murphy. This photo is appropriate when you remember that Pete Clute joined the co-editor and publisher of this book Donna Ewald, in a book about the 1915 Exposition entitled *San Francisco Invites The World* (Chronicle Books, San Francisco, 1991). The Palace of Fine Arts is the only building left standing from that Exposition.

above

Gold Coast Bulletin, Australia, January 4, 1979. Photo of Geoff Russell with racehorse Earthquake McGoon named after the club. Geoff is on the right. Russell really enjoys jazz and loved to join Turk in a duet of duck calls.

right

Flyer for the St. Louis Ragtime Festival June 11-17, 1979.

below

Photo of Golden State Jazz Band taken by Ed Lawless, June 17, 1978. l-r: Bob Mielke, Ev Farey, Hal Smith, Carl Lunsford, Bill Napier and Hank Bartels.

left

Norma Teagarden. In her San Francisco Examiner column (May 14, 1985) Cyra McFadden said: "...down-home, classy, Miss Norma has been a working musician since age 14. Her driving left hand could pull a freight train."

right

Preservation Hall Jazz Band at "the Hall" in New Orleans, circa 1980's. The sign that is partially blocked indicates requests for traditional jazz tunes cost $1.00 and for *The Saints* $5.00. The tuba player and band leader/manager Allan Jaffe, died way too young. He was a pleasant person to know and did much for jazz. Band personnel l-r: Cie Frazier, Frank Demond, Percy Humphrey, Allan Jaffe, Willie Humphrey, Narvin Kimball and Sing Miller. For more information on this unusual group, which gained prominence in the 1960s, the best source is Bill Carter's book *Preservation Hall* (Norton & Co., New York, 1991).

left

Photograph by Jim Goggin of an oil portrait of Monte Ballou which was in Turk Murphy's garage. Monte was the leader of the Castle Jazz Band and worked with the Murphy Band. It is difficult to hear the tune : *I've Been Floating Down That Old Green River* without thinking of Monte. Monte died in 1992 at the age of 89.

below

The Salty Dogs Jazz Band, circa 1980. A group well worth hearing. l-r: Mike Wallbridge, John Cooper, Jack Kuncl, Wayne Jones, Carol Leigh, Lew Green, Tom Bartlett, Kim Cusack.

below

Ray Skjelbred, circa 1980s. Before moving to the San Francisco Bay Area Ray worked with various bands in the Seattle area as well as studying with Johnny Wittwer. He has recorded with Turk Murphy and others plus a solo LP.

right

Photo of Burt Bales by Gary Schroeder, December, 1980. Lizzie Miles remarked when she first heard Burt, "He's the closest to Jelly Roll of anyone I've heard." Gary Schroeder was on the board of the San Francisco Traditional Jazz Foundation and has an extensive record collection. He donated thousands of records and hundreds of photos to the Foundation.

left

Burt Bales calling card for Dick's at the Beach Bar. (Burt added the reference to the Washington Square Bar & Grill.) Founder and former owner of the Washington Square Bar & Grill Ed Moose recalls the night Burt inadvertently set the piano on fire by letting his cigarette fall inside. Oblivious to the flames he kept on playing. Well-known stride pianist Michael Lipskin doused the flames. You can still hear jazz at the "Washbag" and Ed's new place, Moose's, in San Francisco.

left

Advertisements for Turk Murphy's Band to appear at various See's Candies stores in 1980. Even for a band that works 5-6 days a week, the casual is very important financially. It is also a welcome change of scene.

below

Chuck Huggins, President of See's Candies was and still is responsible for hiring many musicians for casuals, including Turk Murphy and Jim Cullum's Jazz Band. Chuck is on the Board of the San Francisco Traditional Jazz Foundation. Here's Chuck sitting in on drums with Turk Murphy circa 1980.

left

Autographed publicity photo of Jabbo Smith, who appeared at Earthquake McGoon's on August 24, 1980. Cladys "Jabbo" Smith worked with Charlie Johnson and Erskine Tate in the 1920s and recorded with Duke Ellington, Fats Waller as well as his own band. Jabbo was an inventive and copied trumpet player of the late 20s and early 30s.

above

Here's the Hot Jazz Duo (pianist Ron Edgeworth and singer Judith Durham) with Dick Oxtot's Golden Age Jazz Band, circa 1980s. Photograph by Ken Arnold. Personnel l-r: Dick Salzman, Bob Mielke, Dick Oxtot, Jim Goodwin, Bob Helm.

right

Scott Anthony, the intermission banjo player at McGoon's for years photographed by Jack Frost in the 1980s. Scott has a very popular group called The Golden Gate Rhythm Machine.

below

Jimmie Stanislaus, a retired fireman who sang with Turk's band, circa 1970s. Known as *The Yama Yama Man* he had eighty seven professional boxing fights without a loss.

right

Happy 65th Turk! Some of those involved in the party were l-r: Bunky Colman, Jim Goggin, Pancho Lopez, Pete Clute, Ev Farey, Norma Teagarden, Phil Elwood, Lu Watters, Bob Mielke, and Harry Mordecai. On stage Turk, Ed Lawless and Wally Rose. The photographer on the left is Roy Sammartano who with his wife Laverne were faithful followers of the Murphy Band and loved to kick up their heels on the dance floor. Photo by Jim Watt, processed by Ed Lawless, December 16, 1980.

left

Tent card for Sippie Wallace who appeared at McGoon's with Jim Dapogny's Little Chicago Jazz Band on September 15, 1980. Sippie, born Beulah Thomas, was the sister of Hersal Thomas the pianist. She recorded in the 1920s and resumed touring in the 1960s. She was known as a fine blues singer who had quite a following. Jim Dapogny is an excellent pianist who is quite knowledgeable about Jelly Roll Morton.

Annie, that jazz street, is back again

above

Annie Street re-dedication. Headline from San Francisco Examiner article by Bill Boldenweck, December 17, 1980.

below left

Flyer about the naming of Annie Street which had been renamed "Mark Twain Lane" a few years prior. The New Orleans Jazz Club of Northern California spearheaded the drive to return the name to Annie Street. The official date of change was December 17, 1980.

below right

Photo of the plaque marking the site of the Dawn Club by Ed Lawless. This was the front cover of the New Orleans Jazz Club News for January of 1981. The event was attended by Turk Murphy, Bob Schulz, Bob Helm, Bill Carroll, Pete Clute, John Gill, Augie Giretto, Peter Tamony, Russ Bennett, Harry Mordecai, Wally Rose and many jazz fans. For a short time the San Francisco Traditional Jazz Foundation's museum was located in what was the Dawn Club. The Dawn Club's site has been reopened as a restaurant named Annie's.

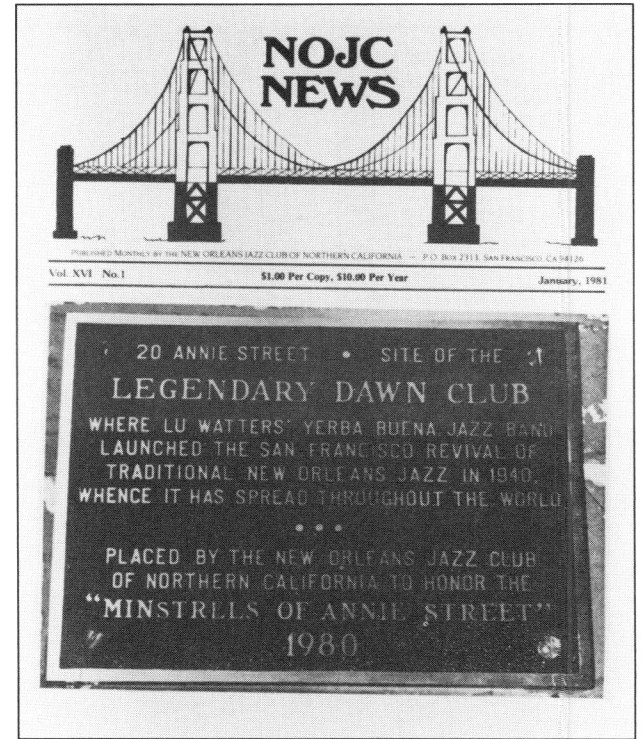

The Great Jazz Revival

above and right

Two cartoons drawn by Russell Myers circa 1979 and 1980.

left

Pat Yankee, Turk Murphy and Pete Clute during Pat's version of *Was I Drunk* taken at the National Ragtime & Traditional Jazz Festival in St Louis, June 20, 1981. Photo by Leslie Johnson, editor of The Mississippi Rag. Pat's husband, Lou Rosenaur, is a great friend to jazz and was a board member of the San Francisco Traditional Jazz Foundation.

below

Pat Yankee and Her Gentlemen of Jazz. A very busy band! Clockwise from bottom: Bill Maginnis, Bill Carlson, Lou Rosenaur, Buddy Powers (sadly, Buddy has passed away since this picture was taken), Shota Osabe, Phil Howe and Pat Yankee. Pat is a truly professional entertainer who is well-liked by more than just jazz purists. She has performed throughout Europe and America.

below

The Spasm Band playing *Razzy Dazzy* written by Turk Murphy in 1982 for his musical *Storyville* that contains some music that is quite moving. Jim Goggin and his wife Maria dined frequently with Turk and Harriet Murphy and liked to hear about the progress of *Storyville* as well as numerous other anecdotes about jazz. l-r: John Gill, Bob Schulz, Lynn Zimmer, Bill Carroll and Turk Murphy, June 1982.

right

Ernie Carson with the Salty Dogs, June 1982. Shown are l-r; John Cooper, Ernie, Jack Kuncl, and Lew Green, the leader.

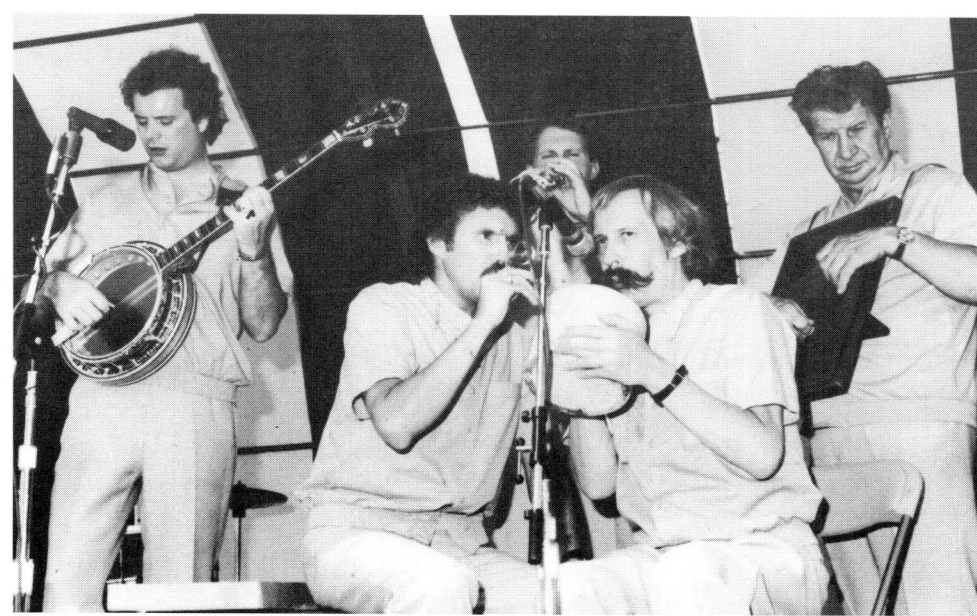

above

Sign announcing that Turk's band will be moving to Pier 39 in San Francisco. Photo by Gary Schroeder.
This was the final home of Earthquake McGoon's. They just could not handle the rent and even though the Pier 39 people tried to help the rent just accumulated until they had to shut it down.

left

Photo of Harry Gold, circa 1980s. His Pieces of Eight Band is still going strong. He is an energetic bass sax player who has had his own band for more years than he would like to recall. He said that when the Jazz Man recordings of the Yerba Buena Jazz Band came to England they had a profound impact on British musicians. This was true of musicians around the world. (The Swedish Barfota Jazzmen led by Claes Ringqvist are great fans of the music specializing in Bunk Johnson).

right

Max Morath. An exremely popular pianist, Morath blends music, humor, history, and satire into his one-man performances. He covers ragtime music from the 1890s through the 1920s.

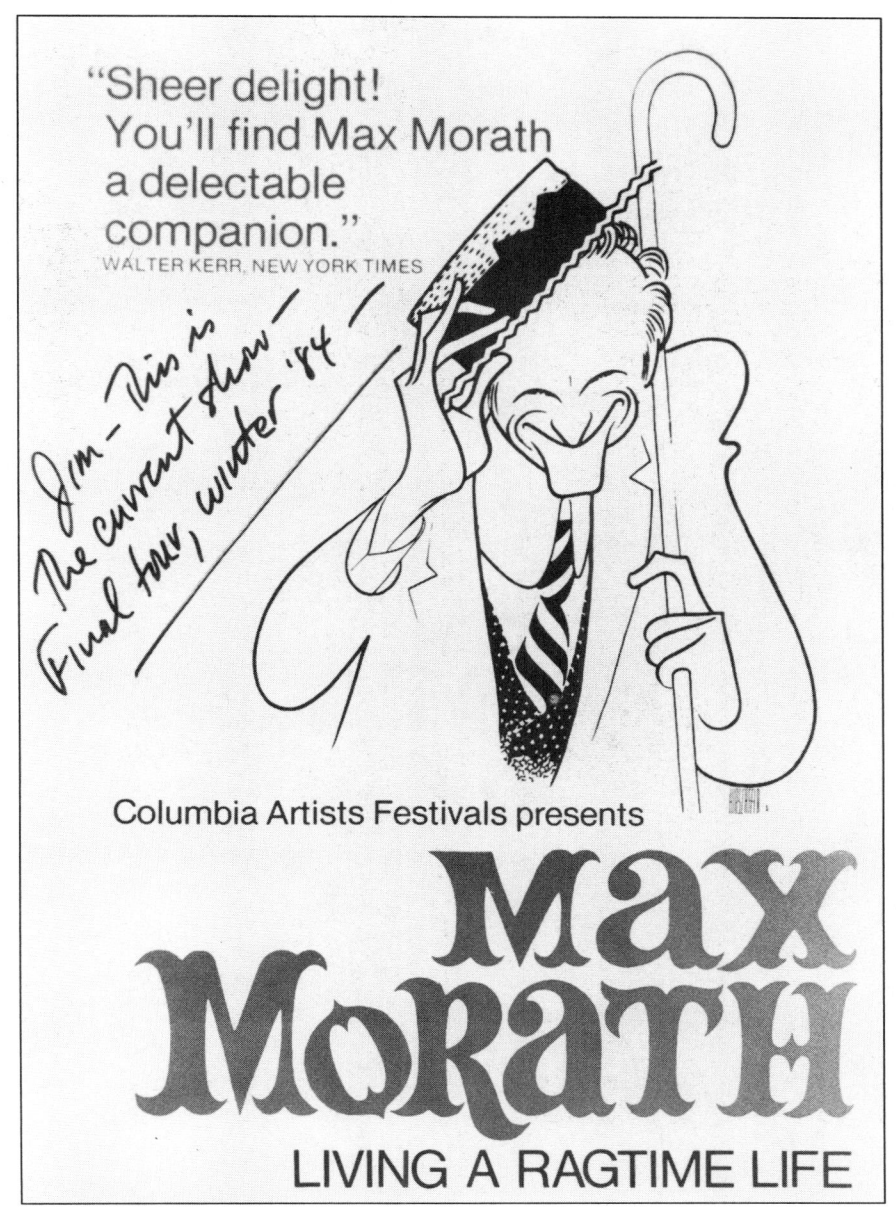

opposite

Photo of Lom Le Goullon at the Goggin's, March 1983. Lom's hand is on a photograph of Bob Helm in front of Lom's 1950s painting of Bob Helm. Do we need to repeat that? Lom's fabulous drawings and paintings as well as album covers related to jazz circa 1950s and 1960s. He also decorated night clubs and the piano at the Italian Village. Photo of Lom by Jim Goggin.

right

Photo of Bob Helm in front of Lom's painting.

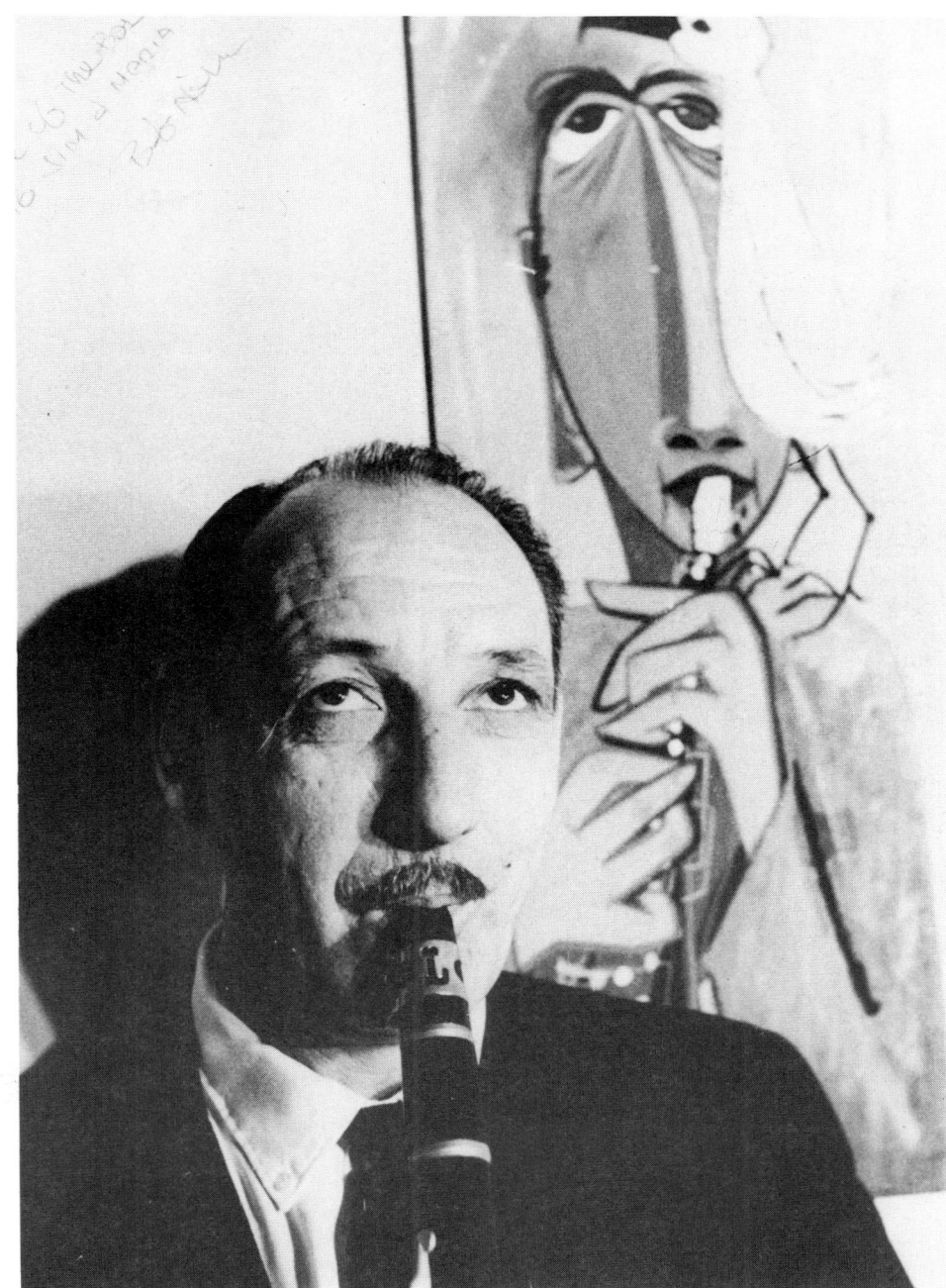

right

Billy Newman Day at the South Bay Traditional Jazz Society meeting in Sunnyvale, March 25, 1984. The San Francisco Traditional Jazz Foundation had a photo display honoring Billy who had worked with the Firehouse Five Plus Two, Turk Murphy, Dude Martin, Johnny Mercer, Bob Scobey, Jack Teagarden and on and on. Here are Billy and Anita Newman in front of a portion of the display. It was not uncommon for Squire Girsback to leave personal belongings with the Newman's when he was touring with Louis Armstrong. One time he was in Germany and it turned quite cold so he wrote the Newman's asking for his camel hair sport coat and overcoat. The Newman's immediately mailed him a home-made moth. Squire wrote back "very funny, but I'm freezing my ass off here in Germany, quit fooling around and send the coats!"

below

Maria Goggin at the Foundation's desk on March 25, 1984 for Billy Newman's Day. Photo by Jim Goggin. Maria, wife of Jim Goggin, helped to organize their collection of jazz memorabilia which they donated to the San Francisco Traditional Jazz Foundation.

below left

The San Francisco Traditional Jazz Foundation's first record was of Pat Yankee. The second LP they issued was *The Two Sides of Wally Rose* Costs of the record production were paid in full by jazz fans Fred and Pat Terry, circa 1988.

below right

Photo of Jim Maihack in a one-man jazz band recording session, May 31, 1989. Jim, a superb musician, is quite at home with various instruments. He has been with numerous bands including Turk Murphy and Rosie O'Grady's. Photo by Charlie Prehn.

right

An excerpt from Herb Caen's column in the San Francisco Chronicle November 13, 1989 in which he mentions the deaths of Burt Bales and Lu Watters. His reference to Burt and Lu being history "chapters, not footnotes" was classic and so very true.

... And jazz in S.F. may not be dead but it's dying fast. The ragtime pianist, Burt Bales, and the legendary "Frisco Jazz" trumpeter, Lu Watters, are now history. Chapters, not footnotes ...

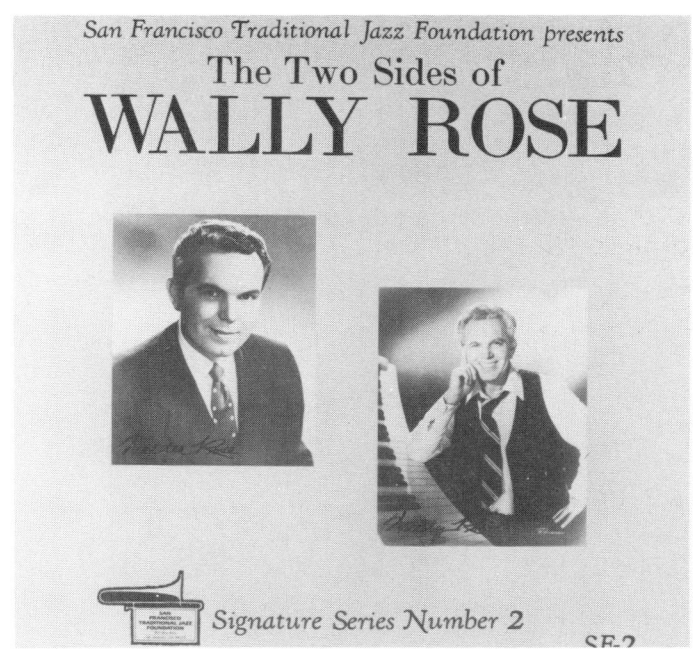

right

Turk's last home base, the Fairmont Hotel's New Orlean's Room where he opened on September 11, 1984.

S.F. Jazz Great Turk Murphy Dies at 71

A Eulogy in Celebration of Turk Murphy's Life
By
Philip Elwood - Music Critic, San Francisco Examiner
MEMORIAL SERVICES - GRACE EPISCOPAL CATHEDRAL - JUNE 5, 1987

Philip Elwood, one of Turk Murphy's oldest friends and supporters, is participating at this moment in his youngest son's high school graduation ceremonies.

He asked that these remarks be read in his absence . . .

It is altogether fitting that this tribute to Turk -- whose band, more than any other, put San Francisco on the jazz world's musical map -- should be held in this house of the Lord.

Turk loved this Cathedral, despite its atrocious acoustics, as he loved all of San Francisco. He played here often; not far down the hill on Clay Street he and his San Francisco Jazz Band hit their musical peak at Earthquake McGoon's in the 1960's and 70's.

His playing days ended, only a few weeks ago, as he and his band played their regular gig in the Fairmont Hotel -- where, also, his grand 70th Birthday Party was held.

Turk acquired me as a wide-eyed 14 year old fan -- a record-collecting, piano-playing, jazz enthusiast -- in 1941. As the years swung along we gradually realized that our mutual love of the "real and righteous jazz" and of San Francisco had brought us very tightly together.

Turk was more than just a trombonist, singer, composer, bandleader -- and stammering raconteur; he was, in the finest tradition of his calling (and of this sanctuary, too) -- both a teacher and a preacher.

By his playing he spread his musical gospel -- in his selection of tunes and in his own compositions he displayed his dedication to the free musical spirit of the earliest New Orleans jazzmen-as well as to the more rowdy and ragtimish sounds of San Francisco in the early years of this century.

Turk never lost his spirit, his enthusiasm -- and it was contagious. In New York City, in January, when thousands of "moldy figs" gathered for a "Turk Murphy at Carnegie Hall" show (which was really one last hurrah for Turk -- and we all knew it) we were overwhelmed at the turn out.

Turk, in the early 1950s, had brought his San Francisco Jazz Band to Manhattan -- he acquired on that trip and on only a couple of other tours, a following that remained dedicated to him and his music for the rest of his life.

In fact, the geographical identification of "San Francisco" in his band's name came to be the definition of Turk's sounds -- "San Francisco Jazz -- in the New Orleans Tradition".

Throughout the world, the name Turk Murphy meant San Francisco jazz; there was seldom a Murphy performance -- and I was in on hundreds of them -- that someone in the audience didn't approach Turk, respectfully, to say "hello, -- I'm from England, or Argentina, Italy, Australia."

San Francisco has lost not only its preeminent Jazz Ambassador and symbol -- with Turk's passing from the scene it has also lost yet another link with its rich, vernacular musical past.

Turk knew and loved San Francisco -- and he gave to it (usually without fee) far, far more than he received.

He enriched the musical lives of millions; for a few of us his personal warmth, good humor and friendship extended to our innermost soul.

Turk loved the old gospel-spirituals -- they were as much a part of old New Orleans music as were the blues and stomps. "50 Miles of Elbow Room", "When I Move to the Sky", "Just a Closer Walk With Thee", and many, many more.

And so, I will bid my farewell in kind --

"Flee as the bird", Turk -- you made the long, lonesome road smoother for all of us.

left

The eulogy for Turk was beautifully written by Phil Elwood and read by long-time friend Chuck Huggins. Headline from a San Francisco Chronicle article by Maitland Zane.

left

Photo of Lu Watters on cover of a magazine issued by the King Cresol Jazz Band of Japan, October 10, 1991.

below

A CD recording by the King Cresol Jazz Band done as a tribute to Lu Watters, 1991.

below

The Minstrels of Annie Street. Standing l-r: John Gill, Bob Schulz, Ray Skjelbred, Phil Howe. Kneeling l-r: Carl Lunsford, Bill Carroll.

right above

From Herb Caen's column, San Francisco Chronicle, March 31, 1992 which referred to John Gill's Band at the New Delhi, San Francisco.

right below

From Herb Caen's column, San Francisco Chronicle, January 19, 1993.

ONLY IN S.F., sort of more or less: A world-class Dixieland band playing in an East Indian restaurant in the Tenderloin. That was Fri. night at the New Delhi, which was packed with toe-tappers and fingersnappers, among them a cherubic Walter Cronkite, a great fan of Frisco Jazz. The moments he spent playing washboard with Turk Murphy at the dear departed Earthquake McGoon's were "the high point of my life, to date," said the Cronk. The band, the Minstrels of Annie St., had a wonderful sound, from cornetist Bob Schultz's Muggsy Spanier wah-wah to the rich tuba of Bill Carroll ...

AFTER dinner, a few of us had a nightcap in Johnny Apple's study and listened to his favorite music — the "Frisco Jazz" of Clancy Hayes, Bob Scobey and Turk Murphy. A man of excellent taste, Apple. I first met him in London, where he lived in Eaton Place, and as I walked toward it I could hear Scobey's blasting trumpet a mile away.

left

Charlie Bornemann and the Yacht Club Resort Hotel Band at Disney World, Florida. l-r: Charlie Bornemann, Greg Barolet, Peter Vrionides and Anthony Dixon. Photo by Harry Grouch taken on March 23, 1993. Charlie is a fine trombone player and was a close friend of Turk Murphy. He is heard on over fifty albums and is one of only two trombonists ever to be a guest artist on a Turk Murphy album.

bottom left

South Frisco Jazz Band. Vince Saunders, banjo, Leon Oakley, cornet, Dan Comins, cornet, Mike Baird, clarinet, Rob Rhodes, piano, Jim Snyder, trombone, Bob Rann, tuba, Bob Raggio, washboard. (Percussionist is currently Lloyd Byassee). Photo by Brenda Oakley.

bottom right

Cocktail napkin from the Gold Dust Lounge in San Francisco which is about the only place in town that employs banjo players on a full-time basis. Musicians who have worked there include Pete Clute, Bob Franklin, Carl Lunsford and Jim Maihack.

right

An Orlando Florida spot for jazz is Church Street Station, home for Rosie O'Grady's Good Time Jazz Band. Here's a publicity shot that asks the musical question: Where's Jim Buchmann?

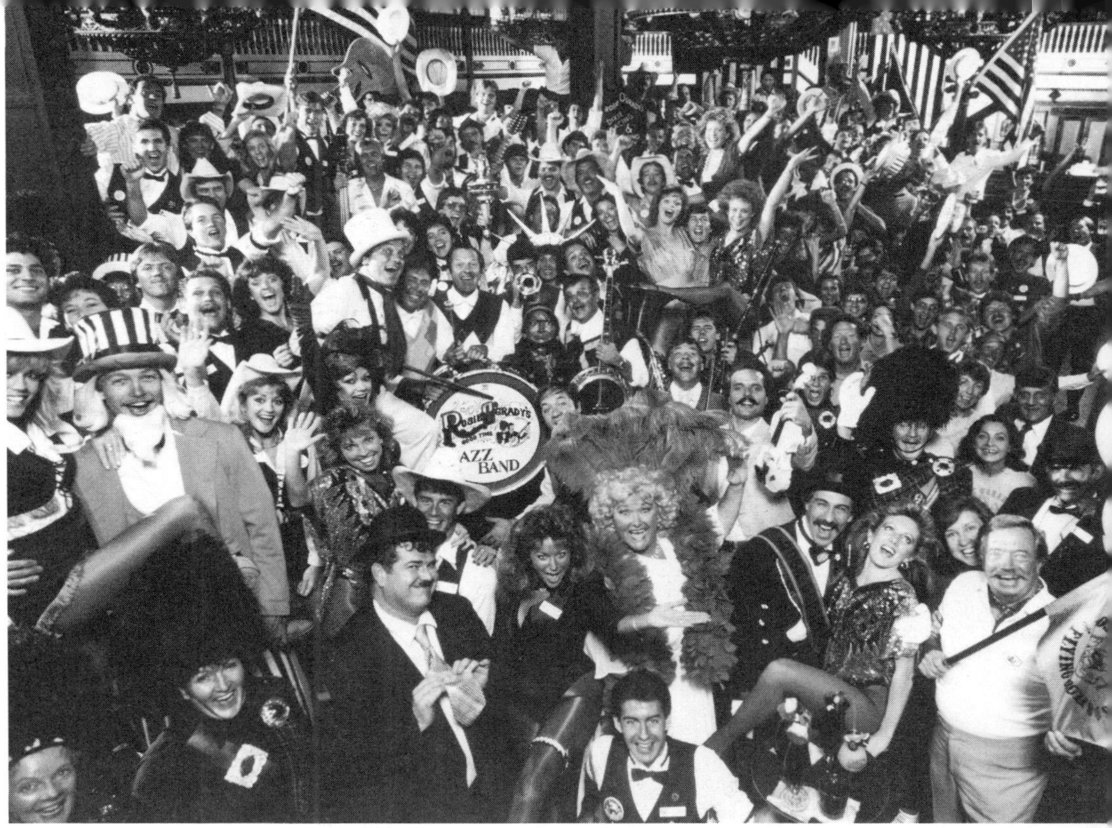

below

To help you find Jim, here's his photograph.

"Gentleman Jim" Buckmann

top left

At Pete and Carol Clute's house in Aptos, California March 1993. Pete with his brother Cedric. Cedric ran the Magic Cellar at McGoon's and when asked nicely would come upstairs and sing *She's Just a Cousin of Mine* with Turk's Band.

bottom left

Personnel of The Natural Gas Jazz Band l-r: Back Row: Bob Murphy, Carl Lunsford, Ed Zimbrick, Dave Lewis and Warren Perry. Front Row: Pete Clute and Phil Crumley.

right

Bob Mielke's New Bearcats. L-r rear: Pete Allen, bass, Tony Marcus, guitar. Middle: Bob Mielke, trombone, Ray Skjelbred, piano, Jack Minger, trumpet, Don Marchant, drums. Foreground: Bill Napier, clarinet.

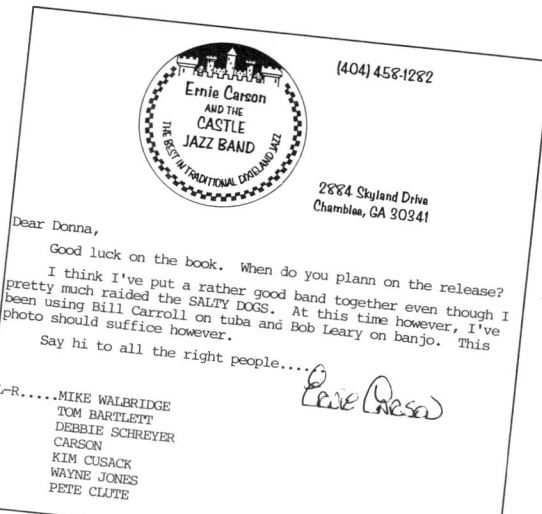

Dear Donna,

Good luck on the book. When do you plann on the release?

I think I've put a rather good band together even though I pretty much raided the SALTY DOGS. At this time however, I've been using Bill Carroll on tuba and Bob Leary on banjo. This photo should suffice however.

Say hi to all the right people....

Ernie Carson

L-R.....MIKE WALBRIDGE
TOM BARTLETT
DEBBIE SCHREYER
CARSON
KIM CUSACK
WAYNE JONES
PETE CLUTE

left

Another full-time band that is really worth listening to is The Uptown Lowdown Jazz Band which is based in Seattle, Washington. Personnel are l-r: standing: Rose Marie Barr, Bert Barr, John Goodrich, Ed Krenz, Bill Kick, Dave Brown. Kneeling: Paul Woltz and Dan Marcus.

With this instrumentation it would be fun to hear them play *Get It Right*. This band has been around for twenty-one years and are still adding to their book. Turk Murphy greatly admired the Barrs for trying to keep a band working full-time. Photo circa 1990s.

right

Photo of the nucleus of the Magnolia Jazz Band. Robbie Schlosser, bass and leader, Bill Napier, clarinet and Paul Mehling, guitar. They often add trumpet, trombone, piano, and drums. (Paul was a student of Billy Newman.)

below and right

Candid photos of the Sacramento Jazz Jubilee which is sponsored by the Sacramento Traditional Jazz Society. The very first festival featured the Turk Murphy Band who did not charge the jazz society and thus, provided them with some funds for the next year. From that modest beginning the Memorial Day weekend festival has become the largest festival in America with audiences in excess of 100,000. A great time is guaranteed.

above

Annual Dixieland Monterey program, March 5-7, 1993. This is a very well-run jazz festival.

left

The Jim Cullum Jazz Band, circa 1992. l-r: Eddie Torres, Mike Pittsley, Alan Vaché (current clarinetist is Brian Ogilvie), Jim Cullum, John Sheridan and Don Mopsick. This full time and very popular band has been in San Antonio since 1962. Jim Cullum and Chuck Huggins were the "guiding lights" in putting together a Turk Murphy appearance at Carnegie Hall. You can listen to Jim's band on *Riverwalk, Live From The Landing*, produced by Pacific Vista Productions, Texas Public Radio, and Jim Cullum. Distributed nationwide by American Public Radio.

right

In 1994 The San Francisco Board of Supervisors passed a resolution to have a street named after Turk Murphy. Turk Murphy Lane is located between Stockton and Powell Streets at Vallejo. Charles Campbell, Supervisor Sue Bierman and President of the Parking and Traffic Commission Jack Molinari were among those who made it happen. Pictured on this page clockwise from the top are: Jack Molinari; Bob and Kay Helm; Lou Rosenaur and Phil Elwood; (l-r) Jim Maihack (barely visible), Bob Mielke, Bob Schulz, Pat Yankee, Carl Lunsford, Leon Oakley, Bob Helm, Charles Campbell, Harry Mordecai, Norma Teagarden, Dottie Lawless and Scott Anthony (kneeling); John Friedlander, husband of Norma Teagarden, Norma, Wally Rose and Supervisor Bierman; Carson Murphy and his mother Harriet. Photos taken at the dedication, March 18, 1994, by Donna Ewald. This page was our choice to end the book and demonstrates the staying power of traditional jazz.

SELECTED BIBLIOGRAPHY

by Jim Goggin

The San Francisco Traditional Jazz Foundation has thousands of books pertaining to music and from that collection I have prepared a list that represents a good starting point for those interested in learning more about the jazz revival.

Armstrong, Louis, *Satchmo*; New York, Prentice Hall (1954)
Bechet, Sidney, *Treat It Gentle*; New York, Da Capo Press (1975)
Blesh, Rudi and Harriet Janis, *They All Played Ragtime*; New York, Knopf (1950)
Carter, Bill, *Preservation Hall*; New York, Norton & Co. (1991)
Chilton, John, *Who's Who of Jazz*; Philadelphia, Chilton Books (1978)
Collier, James Lincoln, *The Making of Jazz*; Boston, Houghton Mifflin Co (1978)
Condon, Eddie and Richard Gehman, *Eddie Condon's Treasury of Jazz*; New York, Dial Press (1956)
Dexter, Dave, Jr., *The Jazz Story*; New Jersey, Prentice Hall (1954)
Eckland, K.O., *Jazz West 1945 to 1985*; Carmel, Cypress (1986)
Feather, Leonard, *The Encyclopedia of Jazz*; New York, Horizon Press (1955)
Gleason, Ralph, *Jam Session*; New York, Horizon Press (1955)
Goggin, Jim, *Turk Murphy—Just for the Record*; Berkeley, SFTJF (1982)
Grossman, William L. and Jack W. Farrell, *The Heart of Jazz*; New York, New York University Press (1956)
Harris, Rex, *Jazz*; New York, Grossett & Dunlop (1955)
Hadlock, Richard, *Jazz Masters of the Twenties*; New York, Collier Books (1974)
Hentoff, Nat and Nat Shapiro, *Hear Me Talkin' To Ya*; New York, Holt, Rinehart and Winston (1955)
Hodes, Art and Chadwick Hansen, *Selections form the Gutter*; Berkeley, University of California Press (1977)
Keepnews, Orrin and Bill Grauer, Jr., *A Pictorial History of Jazz*; New York, Bonanza Books (1981)
Lomax, Alan, *Mister Jelly Roll*; New York, Da Capo Press (1978)
Oliver, Paul, *Blues Fell This Morning*; New York, Horizon Press (1961)
Panassie, Hugues and Madelaine Gautier, *Dictionary of Jazz*; London, Cossellt Co. (1956)
Ramsey, Frederic, Jr., *Been Here and Gone*; New Jersey, Rutgers University Press (1960)
Ramsey, Frederic, Jr., *Jazzmen*; New York, Harcourt, Brace & Company (1939)
Sales, Grover, *Jazz: America's Classical Music*; New Jersey, Prentice Hall (1984)
Scobey, Jan, *He Rambled 'till the Cancer Cut Him Down*; Northridge, CA Pal Publishing (1976)
Scott, Toni Lee, *A Kind of Loving*; New York, World Publishing Co. (1970)
Schacter, James D., *Piano Man*; Chicago, Jaynar Press (1975)
Shapiro, Nat and Nat Hentoff, *The Jazz Makers*; New York, Rinehart & Co. (1957)
Stearns, Marshall, *The Story of Jazz*; New York, Oxford University Press (1956)
Stoddard, Tom, *Jazz on the Barbary Coast*; Storyville Publications and Co. Ltd. (1982)
Waldo, Terry, *This is Ragtime*; New York, Macmillan Co. (1967)
Williams, Martin, *Jazz Masters of New Orleans*; New York, Macmillan Co. (1967)
Wilson, John S., *Jazz: The Transition Years, 1940–1960*; New York, Appleton-Century, Crofts (1966)

DISCOGRAPHY

In approaching a selective recordings list, I thought it appropriate to have three basic divisions: (1) Examples of recordings that were the basis for the jazz revival (Armstrong, Morton, Oliver, etc.). (2) Some recordings made by the revival musicians. (3) Finally, some recordings made after the first wave of revivalists.

This list is brief and the recordings, for the most part, should be available. If you experience difficulty finding any of these, you are welcome to write to me, including an addressed, stamped envelope, and I will try to help you. Jim Goggin, P. O. Box 15, Twain Harte, CA 95383

Artist	Title	Format	Number	Label
Various	New Orleans	1*	781700-2	Atlantic
Various	History of Classic Jazz	1	VDJ-1575	Riverside
Louis Armstrong	Giants of Jazz Series	1,2,3	JO1	Time-Life
Burt Bales	On The Waterfront	2	CVLP-6010	Cavalier
Bay City Jazz Band	Golden Days	2	S-10053	Good Time Jazz
Jim Cullum	Super Satch	3	C-1148	Stomp Off
Down Home Jazz Band	Hambone Kelly Favorites	2	SOS-1171	Stomp Off
Frisco Jazz Band	A Good Man…	2	DC-12005	Dawn Club
John Gill–Sunset Five	Down Home Blues	2	SOS-1126	Stomp Off
Clancy Hayes	Swingin' Minstrel	2	M-12050	Good Time Jazz
King Cresol	Tribute to Lu Watters	1	BPCD-91086	Build (Japan)
Magnolia Jazz Band	Red Onion Blues	2	SOS-1016	Stomp Off
Bob Mielke	The Bearcats	1	SF-3	SF Traditional Jazz Foundation
Max Morath	The Best of Scott Joplin	1	VCD-39/40	Vanguard
Jelly Roll Morton	Giants of Jazz Series	1,2,3	JO7	Time-Life
Turk Murphy	Favorites	1	FCD60-011	Good Time Jazz
Natural Gas Jazz Band	SF Jazz of Watters and Murphy	1	V.3	Natural Gas
King Oliver	1923–1931	2	C89/6	Joker (Italy)
Kid Ory	Creole Jazz Band	2	L12022	Good Time Jazz
Dick Oxtot	Down in Honky Tonk Town	2	4010	Arhoolie
Wally Rose	The Two Sides of	2	SF-2	SF Traditional Jazz Foundation
Salty Dogs	The Original	2	6437-128	Jazz & Jazz (Australia)
Bob Schulz	Frisco Jazz Band	1	JCD-206	Jazzology
Bob Scobey	Favorites	1	FCD60-010	Good Time Jazz
Ray Skjelbred	Stompin' 'em Down	2	SOS-1124	Stomp Off
Jim Snyder	Music of Roy Palmer	2	SOS-1068	Stomp Off
South Frisco Jazz Band	Live From Earthquake McGoon's	2	SOS-1027	Stomp Off
Uptown Lowdown Jazz Band	Business in F	1	BDJ-CD2	Dan Jazz
Lu Watters–Bunk Johnson	Bunk & Lu	2	L12024	Good Time Jazz
Lu Watters	Yerba Buena Jazz Band	1	4GTJCD-4409	Good Time Jazz
Turk Murphy Jazz Band with Wally Rose and Lu Watters	Blues on Bodega Bay	1	MMRC-CD-8	Merry Makers Recording Co.
Johnny Wittwer	Piano Rags	2	SLP58	Stinson
Pat Yankee	Pat Yankee	2,3	SF-1	SF Traditional Jazz Foundation

*(1) Compact Disc (2) LP–12 inch (3) Cassette

left

Jim Goggin and Peter Clute.
Photo by Maria Goggin.

Jim is a retired banker. A long time jazz fan, he founded the San Francisco Traditional Jazz Foundation and has been actively involved in producing jazz recordings. He also wrote *Turk Murphy-Just For the Record* and *Bob Scobey, A Bibliography and Discography* as well as numerous jazz related articles.

Pete was the long-time, much loved piano player in the Turk Murphy Band and was a co-founder of Earthquake McGoon's in San Francisco. He was a student of the famous Wally Rose and he continues to compose, arrange and perform jazz with the Natural Gas Jazz Band. He wrote (with Donna Ewald) a book on the 1915 Exposition *San Francisco Invites the World*.